The Complete Fix-It-Yourself Home Appliances Handbook

The Complete Fix-It-Yourself Home Appliances Handbook

James Edward Keogh

PARKER PUBLISHING COMPANY, INC.
West Nyack, N.Y.

Library of Congress Cataloging in Publication Data

Keogh, James Edward
    The complete fix-it-yourself home appliances hand-
book.

    Includes index.
    1. Household appliances, Electric--Maintenance and
repair--Amateurs' manuals. I. Title.
TK9901.K46   643'.6   79-457
ISBN 0-13-159947-X

Printed in the United States of America

Your Guide to Inexpensive, Timesaving Appliance Repairs

You can achieve professional appliance repairs without paying high prices and without wasting time taking your appliances to repair shops or waiting for the repair person to arrive (provided you can find one who will stop by at *your* convenience). In this easy-to-follow book, *all* the information you need to make safe, professional electrical and mechanical repairs is presented in a unique and thoroughly tested format.

Each section contains:

- components in an exploded view that give you the whole picture before you disassemble the unit. Thus, you will know that every part is in the right position when you reassemble the appliance.

- a complete description of how the appliance operates. This provides essential information so you will know it is a *safe* repair.

- unique troubleshooting flow charts that cover every malfunction an appliance may have, making for the difference between a professional and a non-professional repair job.

- testing and repair procedures that show the quick and

easy step-by-step methods used by professionally trained repair persons.

Remember when the clothes washer suddenly stopped in the middle of a full load of wash? It probably took several days, if not a week or more, before the repair person could make an appointment to visit your home. Wouldn't you like to have the clothes washer, or any other appliance, back in working order quickly? You may think appliance repairs are difficult or dangerous, but they really are not, as long as you have concise information that you can understand and follow.

This book is packed with all the essential, practical information you need, and the troubleshooting flow charts will make locating the problem quick, easy, and safe. The step-by-step instructions also show you *when* to make certain tests and *how* to make each test. You do not have to wade through pages and pages to find the proper professional troubleshooting and test procedures. Each test is presented in short, specific, clearly illustrated steps so you can find the problem quickly. This will not only help you make fast repairs but will simplify the routine maintenance all appliances need.

Even if you know nothing about how an appliance operates, you will learn the same way the professionals are trained. From the easy-to-read tips on electricity (Appendix A) you will develop the know-how to understand both small and large appliances. Each section begins with a clear description of how the mechanism works, followed by an exploded view of the appliance that identifies its major components. You will be able to understand how the appliance operates and can refer to the exploded view for a clear picture of the operation.

Repairing an appliance can be easy or difficult, depending on the use of a few simple, inexpensive tools. In this book you will learn what tools you need and, equally important, how to use these tools in the right way, the professional way. From the use of a simple glow light to the basic volt-ohmmeter, proper use will make the repair easy and effortless.

No previous knowledge of tools or mechanics is required to turn your appliance into a working servant again.

Save money and time by being able to repair and maintain all your electric appliances. This book shows you how to master all the necessary skills easily and safely.

James Edward Keogh

Contents

Your Guide to Inexpensive, Timesaving Appliance
   Repairs 5
Section I   How to Repair Small Appliances 13
   How Blenders Work (14)
   How a Coffeemaker works (26)
   How a Cooker Works (34)
   How Electric Blankets Work (40)
   How an Electric Broiler Works (48)
   How the Electric Can Opener Works (56)
   How an Electric Clock Works (66)
   How Electric Curlers Work (74)
   How an Electric Corn Popper Works (84)
   How an Electric Knife Works (92)
   How Electric Shavers Work (104)
   How the Electric Toothbrush Works (112)
   How an Electric Fan Works (118)
   How Handheld Hair Dryers Work (128)
   How Heating Pads Work (136)
   How Hot Plates Work (142)
   How the Electric Iron Works (150)
   How the Electric Mixer Works (164)
   How Space Heaters Work (176)
   How a Toaster Works (184)
   How the Vacuum Cleaner Works (196)

Section II   How to Repair Large Appliances ...207
How a Clothes Dryer Works (208)
How a Dehumidifier Works (220)
How a Dishwasher Works (228)
How a Room Air Conditioner Works (238)
How a Humidifier Works (246)
How a Refrigerator Works (254)
How a Sewing Machine Works (264)
How a Stove Works (272)
How a Washing Machine Works (280)
How a Waste Disposer Works (290)
Appendix A   Tips on Home Electricity 296
Things to Know About Electricity (296)
About Amps (297)
How to Prevent Blown Fuses or Circuit Breakers (299)
How to Select the Proper Extension Cords (300)
Appendix B   Tools of the Trade 308
How to Select Tools for Appliance Repair (308)
Supplies Required (312)
Appendix C   Tricks of the Trade 313
Where to Obtain Specs (313)
Tricks to Installing Parts (315)
How to Talk Like a Professional (318)
Index 321

The Complete Fix-It-Yourself Home Appliances Handbook

Section I

How to Repair Small Appliances

As a preliminary step, you will find it helpful to review any printed material that came with your appliance. The specifications and other data could be of assistance in applying repair techniques described in the pages that follow. *Always* follow the proper safety procedures as described in Appendix A.

How Blenders Work

Combining various ingredients to make even the highly demanding culinary wink approval can be somewhat of a chore for the homemaker/chef. A handheld mixer will do the job, but it will also leave a mess of the counter and surrounding areas. To solve such a problem, manufacturers produced the blender, a mixer-like device with a self-contained mixing bowl attached. (See Illustration 1-1.)

The blender operates directly from the motor shaft. Current flows into the motor turning the motor shaft. In turn, movement is given to the blender blade contained in the mixing jar. On the control panel of most blenders exist three sections. There is the on-off switch, speed control selection, and on some blenders a "quick" switch.

As with other appliances, the on-off switch enables power to flow into the system. Through a selection of resistors, current from the switch is regulated before entering the motor. The user, by selecting the speed, is either adding or removing resistance to the current. The more resistance, the slower the motor turns; the less resistance, the faster the motor turns.

To enable short bursts of blending, a "quick" switch is used. This is a button that closes the circuit to allow the motor to turn at a preset speed. The motor will only turn for as long as the button is depressed.

In Summary: Current from the power cord turns the motor shaft which is directly connected to the blender blade. Speed of the motor is controlled by adding and removing resistance to the current by depressing speed control buttons.

Blender

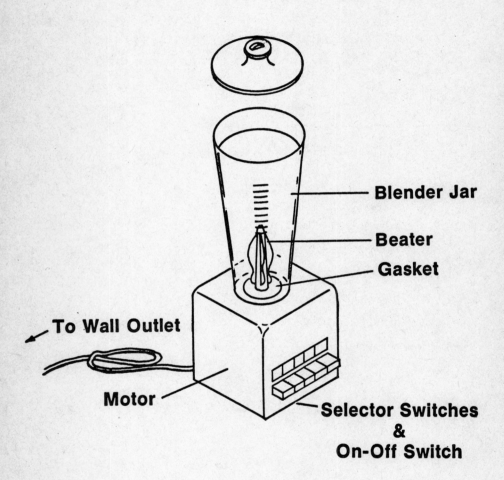

ILLUSTRATION 1-1. *Exploded View of Blender*

DIAGNOSING THE BLENDER

PROBLEMS

Blender Does Not Operate .... page 19

Does Not Operate on All Speeds .... page 21

Blender Is Noisy .... page 23

Blender Bowl Leaks .... page 23

Blender Gives Shocks .... page 25

How to Check Wall Outlet

- Unplug blender.
- Readjust circuit breaker or fuse.
- Plug in appliance that is known to operate properly.
- If fuse continues to blow, check amp rating of other appliances operating on the same power line.
- Total amps per wall outlet should not be more than 15 amps for most home outlets.
- If necessary, turn off appliances until appropriate total amp rate is reached.

How to Check If Blender Is Jammed

- Plug in blender.
- Remove blender bowl.
- Turn on blender and operate.
- Turn off blender.
- Reinstall blender bowl.
- Turn on blender and operate.
- Blender should operate at same speed. If blender operates faster with the blender bowl removed, then the blade drive is jammed.
- Disassemble unit and remove obstruction.
- Reassemble.

How to Check Power Cord

- Unplug blender.
- Preset volt-ohmmeter to RX 1 scale.
- Remove plug from blender.
- Attach jumper wire to blender end of cord. (See Illustration 1-2.)
- Attach volt-ohmmeter probes to power cord prongs.
- Volt-ohmmeter should indicate zero. If not, replace cord.

How to Check Switch

- Unplug blender.
- Remove selection control unit panel.
- Preset volt-ohmmeter probes to switch wire.
- Switch on blender.
- Volt-ohmmeter should indicate zero. If not, clean or replace switch.

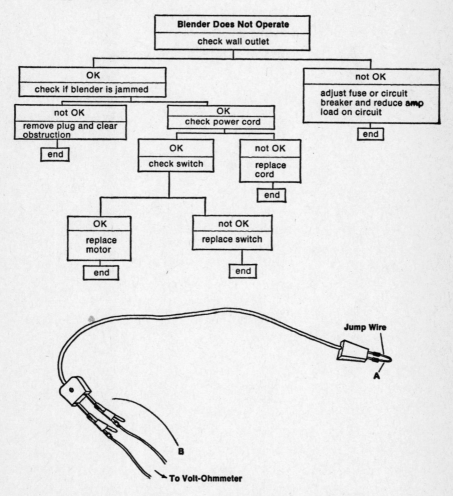

ILLUSTRATION 1-2. *Checking Power Cord*

How to Check Quick Switch

- Unplug blender.
- Remove selection control unit panel.
- Check quick switch contacts.
- If not clean or out of adjustment, make proper repair or replace quick switch.

How to Check for Loose Wires in Speed Control Unit

- Unplug blender.
- Remove selection control unit panel.
- Examine all wire connections.
- If loose wire found, reconnect.

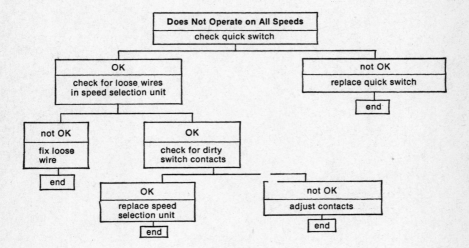

How to Check for Loose Parts

- Unplug blender.
- Remove speed control selection unit.
- Examine for loose parts.
- If loose part not found, remove base of blender.
- Remove motor assembly.
- Examine for loose parts.
- Tighten loose part and reassemble.

How to Check Blender Blade

- Plug in blender.
- Remove blender bowl.
- Turn on blender.
- Turn off blender.
- Reinstall blender bowl.
- Turn on blender.
- If blender is noisy only when blender bowl is installed, remove blender blade assembly and check condition of blender blade.
- Replace blade if necessary.

How to Check Blender Bowl Seal

- Unplug blender.
- Remove blender bowl.
- Remove blade assembly.
- Examine seal for cracks or deformities.
- Replace seal.

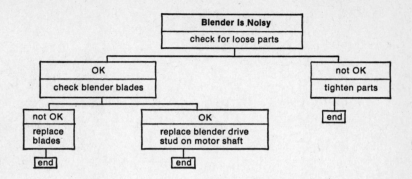

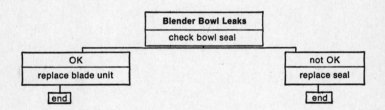

How to Check Power Cord

- Unplug blender.
- Preset volt-ohmmeter to RX 1 scale.
- Remove plug from blender.
- Attach jumper wire to blender end of cord. (See Illustration 1-2.)
- Attach volt-ohmmeter probes to power cord prongs.
- Volt-ohmmeter should indicate zero. If not, replace cord.

How to Check for Short in Blender

- Unplug blender.
- Preset volt-ohmmeter to RX 100 scale.
- Attach one volt-ohmmeter probe to any metal part of blender.
- Connect other volt-ohmmeter probe to power cord.
- Depress each speed control button.
- If volt-ohmmeter indicates high ohms, a short exists and you should take the unit to a professional repair person.

How to Check for Grounded Wire

- Unplug blender.
- Preset volt-ohmmeter to RX 100 scale.
- Remove blender base.
- Attach volt-ohmmeter probe to stud drive.
- Attach volt-ohmmeter probe to power cord.
- Turn on blender (still unplugged).
- Depress slow button.
- Wiggle each wire in blender. If volt-ohmmeter indicates a change (needle moves), the wire that is being touched is grounded and must be repaired

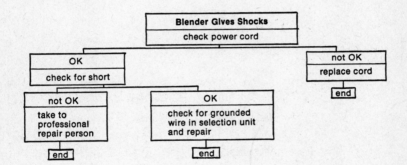

How a Coffeemaker Works

The time-tested method of preparing coffee has been brought up to date. Electric coffeemakers enable the user to simply add coffee and water, turn on a switch, and within a few minutes coffee is brewed. The formula for making coffee in an electric coffeemaker hasn't changed. Water is boiled and filtered through ground coffee beans. An electric coffeemaker combines the ingredients in one mobile unit.(See Illustration 1-3.)

There are two types of coffeemakers in the marketplace—gravity-flow and pump-action—and both operate in a similar manner. Current from the power cord enters a heating element through a thermostat. Resistance of the element wire generates a high enough temperature to boil water. To maintain a constant temperature, the manufacturer installed a bimetal contact or thermostat. As heat from the element increases beyond the desired temperature, the bimetal contact is heated and breaks the circuit. When the element cools below the selected temperature, the contact again completes the circuit.

In the gravity-flow coffeemaker, the water reservoir and heating element are on top of the unit. Water, after boiling, naturally flows through the coffee beans and into the pot. The pump-action coffeemaker differs in that the water reservoir is located on the bottom of the unit with the heating element. As the water boils, a pump feeds the fluid to the top of the coffeemaker, where the hot water drips through the ground beans.

As a normal maintenance procedure, coffeemakers should be cleaned after every daily use.

Heating Element

Water Reservoir

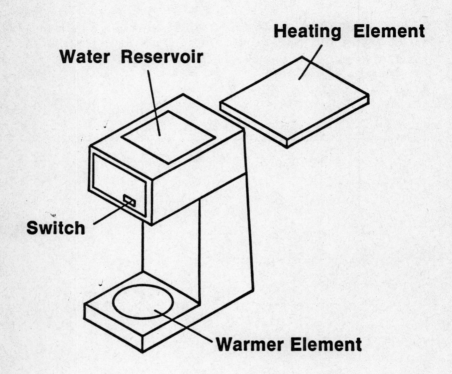

Switch

Warmer Element

ILLUSTRATION 1-3. *Exploded View of Coffeemaker*

DIAGNOSING THE COFFEEMAKER

PROBLEMS

Shocks Received from Coffeemaker .... page 31
Coffee Does Not Keep Warm .... page 31
Water Does Not Flow....................... page 33

How to Check Power Cord

- Unplug coffeemaker.
- Disassemble coffeemaker.
- Preset volt-ohmmeter to RX 1 scale.
- Attach jumper wire to coffeemaker end of power cord. (See Illustration 1-2.)
- Attach volt-ohmmeter probes to power cord prongs.
- Volt-ohmmeter should indicate zero. If not, replace cord.

How to Check for Short Circuit

- Unplug coffeemaker.
- Preset volt-ohmmeter to RX 100 scale.
- Turn on coffeemaker (still unplugged).
- Attach one volt-ohmmeter probe to metal part of coffeemaker.
- Attach other volt-ohmmeter probe to power cord prong.
- Volt-ohmmeter should indicate zero or low. If not, **take** unit to professional repair person or replace unit.

How to Check for Grounded Wire

- Unplug coffeemaker.
- Disassemble coffeemaker.
- Examine all wires for poor connections or burn marks.
- Repair wire or replace unit.

How to Check Switch

- Unplug coffeemaker.
- Disassemble coffeemaker.
- Preset volt-ohmmetr to RX 1 scale.
- Turn on coffeemaker.
- Attach volt-ohmmeter to switch connections.
- Volt-ohmmeter should indicate zero. If not, replace switch.

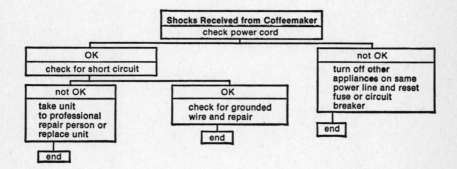

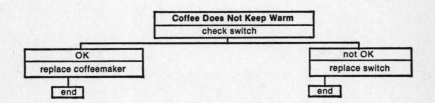

How to Check Wall Outlet

- Unplug coffeemaker.
- Readjust circuit breaker or fuse.
- Plug in appliance that is known to operate properly.
- If fuse continues to blow, check amp rating of other appliances operating on same power line.
- Total amps per wall outlet should not be more than 15 amps for most home outlets.
- If necessary, turn off appliances until appropriate total amp rate is reached.

How to Check for Spout Obstruction

- Unplug coffeemaker.
- Remove all water from unit.
- Invert coffeemaker and clean spout.

How to Check Valve

- Unplug coffeemaker.
- Remove water.
- Disassemble unit.
- Manually examine valve.
- If valve does not move freely, replace valve.

How to Check Switch

- Unplug coffee maker.
- Disassemble coffeemaker.
- Preset volt-ohmmeter to RX 1 scale.
- Turn on coffeemaker.
- Attach volt-ohmmeter to switch connections.
- Volt-ohmmeter should indicate zero. If not, replace switch.

How to Check Power Cord

- Unplug coffeemaker.
- Disassemble coffeemaker.
- Preset volt-ohmmeter to RX 1 scale.
- Attach jumper wire to coffeemaker end of power cord. (See Illustration 1-2.)
- Attach volt-ohmmeter probes to power cord prongs.
- Volt-ohmmeter should indicate zero. If not, replace cord.

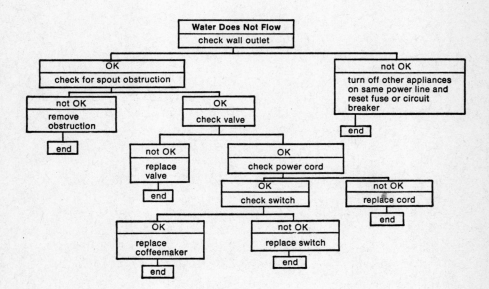

How a Cooker Works

With energy conservation in mind, more and more manufacturers are producing appliances that will reduce the need to turn on the full force of a stove to fry food. The electric cooker has replaced the frying pan for small cooking jobs. (See Illustration 1-4.)

In the base of the frying-pan-shaped cooker is a heating element. Current from the power cord enters the heating element through a detachable control unit. Resistance of the heating element wire to the current generates heat. By controlling the amount of resistance through the use of a control unit, various temperatures can be developed and maintained.

The control unit contains a thermostat. This bimetal device disconnects the circuit, turning off the cooker when the heating element reaches a temperature beyond the one desired. When the element cools, the bimetal contact reconnects the circuit, allowing current to flow again. The selector mechanism fine-tunes the bimetal contact to react at the specific temperature.

The pan end of the cooker can be washed in a dishpan, but not in a dishwasher. Before cleaning be sure the control unit is removed from the pan. Never wash the pan with the control unit connected, for the control unit may be damaged beyond repair. When storing the cooker, place the appliance in a cabinet, never in the oven. Because part of the control unit is made from plastic, heat generated by most ovens, even when the oven is not in use, could melt part of the control unit.

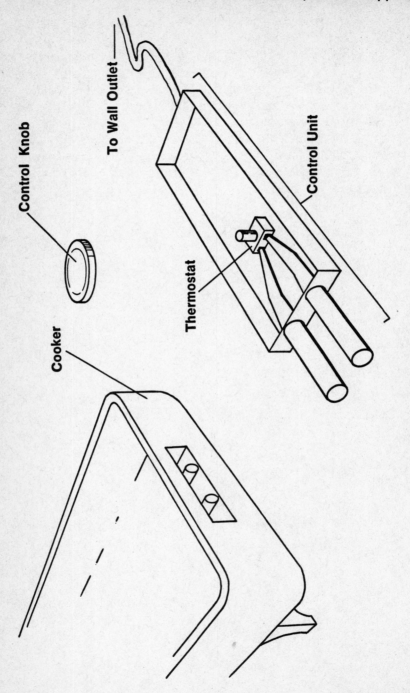

ILLUSTRATION 1-4. *Exploded View of Cooker*

DIAGNOSING THE COOKER

PROBLEMS

Cooker Does Not Operate .... page 39

Shocks Received from Cooker .... page 39

How to Check Wall Outlet

- Unplug cooker.
- Readjust circuit breaker or fuse.
- Plug in appliance that is known to operate properly.
- If fuse continues to blow, check amp rating of other appliances operating on same power line.
- Total amps per wall outlet should not be more than 15 amps for most home outlets.
- If necessary, turn off appliances until appropriate total amp rate is reached.

How to Check Heating Element

- Unplug cooker.
- Unplug control unit.
- Preset volt-ohmmeter to RX 1 scale.
- Attach volt-ohmmeter probes to pan connector.
- Volt-ohmmeter should indicate zero. If not, replace cooker.

How to Check Power Cord

- Unplug cooker.
- Preset volt-ohmmeter to RX 1 scale.
- Disassemble control unit.
- Attach jumper wire to cooker end of power cord. (See Illustration 1-2.)
- Attach volt-ohmmeter probes to power cord prongs.
- Volt-ohmmeter should indicate zero. If not, replace cord.

How to Check for Grounded Wire

- Unplug cooker.
- Unplug control unit.
- Disassemble control unit.
- Examine all wires for poor connections and burn marks and repair wire.

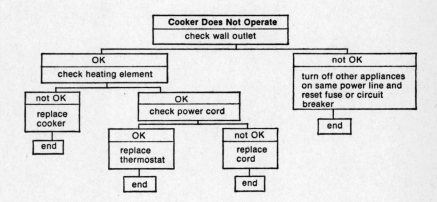

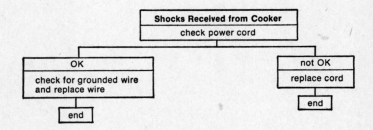

How Electric Blankets Work

In cold winter months when the snow is blowing around outside the house, it always feels good to toss another blanket or two on the bed before turning in for the night. The cold bed is soon warmed by body heat. Then the true test of strength comes in the morning—to get out of the warm bed and into the cold bathroom. With the electric blanket, however, there is need for only one blanket and no need to jump into a cold bed. Getting out of bed, unfortunately, will still be the same.

The electric blanket operates in a manner similar to the space heater. Current from the power cord enters the blanket, heating thin wires sandwiched between two layers of cloth. Heat is generated by the resistance of the small wire to the current. Without controls, internal wires would soon burn up. However, a control system enables the generated heat to remain within the tested limits of the blanket wiring. (See Illustration 1-5.)

Most electric blankets use a double control system, a switch, and a thermostat. The switch enables current to flow to internal blanket wires. The thermostat controls the amount of current in the blanket. A dial selection determines temperature of the blanket. The dial adjusts the thermostat to turn the blanket off when the temperature is at the selected heat. Bimetal contacts automatically respond to a higher than selected temperature and internally disconnect the current. When the bimetal contact cools, the connection is reestablished.

In Summary: Current from the power cord enters and heats thin internal wires in the blanket. In the circuit is a thermostat which, through a bimetal contact, controls and maintains the temperature of the blanket.

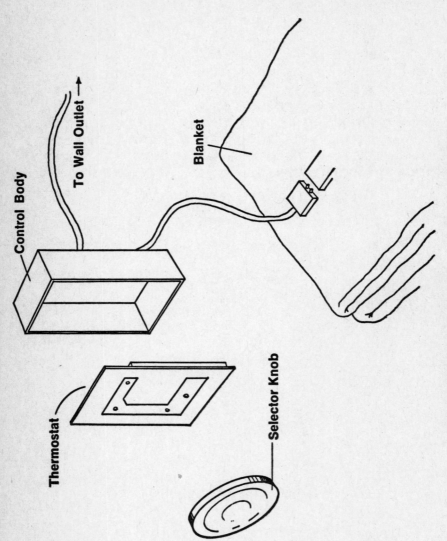

ILLUSTRATION 1-5. *Exploded View of Electric Blanket*

DIAGNOSING THE ELECTRIC BLANKET

PROBLEMS

Blanket Not Heating .... page 45

Temperature Not Steady .... page 47

Shocks Felt When Using Blanket .... page 47

Fuse Blows When Blanket is On .... page 47

How to Check Wall Outlet

- Unplug blanket.
- Readjust circuit breaker or fuse.
- Plug in appliance that is known to operate properly.
- If fuse continues to blow, check amp rating of other appliances operating on same power line.
- Total amps per wall outlet should not be more than 15 amps for most home outlets.
- If necessary, turn off appliances until appropriate total amp rate is reached.

How to Check Heating Element

- Unplug blanket.
- Remove control cord.
- Preset volt-ohmmeter to RX 1 scale.
- Connect volt-ohmmeter probes to male end of plug connected to internal blanket wires.
- Shake blanket.
- Volt-ohmmeter should indicate between 85 and 190 ohms. If not, heating element is broken and should be replaced.

How to Check Power Cord

- Unplug blanket.
- Preset volt-ohmmeter to RX 1 scale.
- Remove plug from blanket.
- Attach jumper wire to blanket end of cord. (See Illustration 1-2.)
- Attach volt-ohmmeter probes to power cord prongs.
- Volt-ohmmeter should indicate zero. If not, replace cord.

How to Check Control Cord

- Unplug blanket.
- Unplug control cord.
- Remove thermostat control body.
- Preset volt-ohmmeter to RX 1 scale.
- Connect jumper wires to control plug cord inside thermostat control body.
- Connect volt-ohmmeter probes to blanket end of control cord.
- Volt-ohmmeter should indicate zero. If not, replace cord.

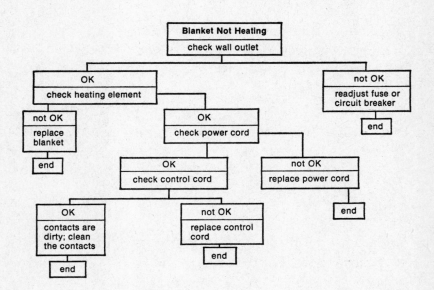

How to Check Thermostat Adjustment

- Unplug blanket.
- Unplug thermostat control unit from blanket.
- Connect jumper wires to female end of thermostat control cord.
- Preset volt-ohmmeter to RX 1 scale.
- Connect volt-ohmmeter probes to power cord.
- Turn on blanket (blanket still unplugged).
- Turn control dial from low to high position.
- Volt-ohmmeter should indicate from high to zero during control dial movement. If not, replace control unit.

How to Check Power Cord

- Unplug blanket.
- Preset volt-ohmmeter to RX 1 scale.
- Remove plug from blanket.
- Attach jumper wire to blanket end of cord. (See Illustration 1-2.)
- Attach volt-ohmmeter probes to power cord prongs.
- Volt-ohmmeter should indicate zero. If not, replace cord.

How to Check for Short in Blanket

- Unplug blanket.
- Unplug thermostat control unit cord from blanket.
- Preset volt-ohmmeter to RX 1 scale.
- Turn on blanket (still unplugged).
- Connect volt-ohmmeter probes to power cord.
- Turn thermostat control unit to high position.
- Volt-ohmmeter must indicate zero. If not, replace thermostat control unit.

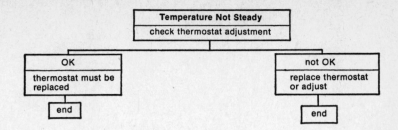

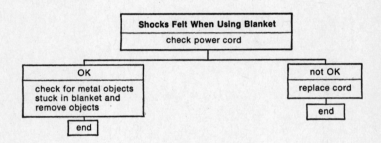

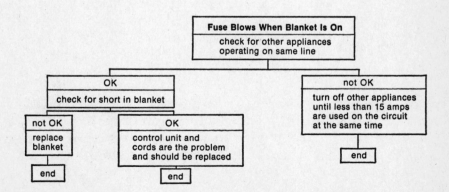

How an Electric Broiler Works

In a move towards increased conservation of natural gas, more and more electric broilers are being used. Parallelling the substitution of hot plates to handle above-stove cooking, electric broilers can cook most of the foods commonly prepared in the oven. (See Illustration 1-6.)

The electric broiler operates in a manner similar to most electric heating appliances. Current from the power cord enters the heating unit, passing through the decreased size of the heating element wire, which creates resistance and generates heat. Usually located near the on-off switch is the thermostat, which is adjusted by temperature selection. A bimetal contact in the thermostat, when heated beyond the selected temperature, will break the circuit and turn off the broiler. When the bimetal contact cools to a temperature below the one selected, the circuit is completed and the broiler is turned on again.

A few tips on the proper care and maintenance of the broiler. After every use, the broiler must be unplugged and left to cool before storage or cleaning. When cleaning, do not allow water to come in contact with the heating elements or the wiring of the broiler. Never place the broiler in a dishpan or dishwasher. Some broilers come equipped with a motor or fan unit. Such an assembly aids in the cooling of the broiler after usage. Every year, the broiler motor should be cleaned and lubricated. When using the broiler, always place the unit on a flat, sturdy surface to prevent the broiler from falling.

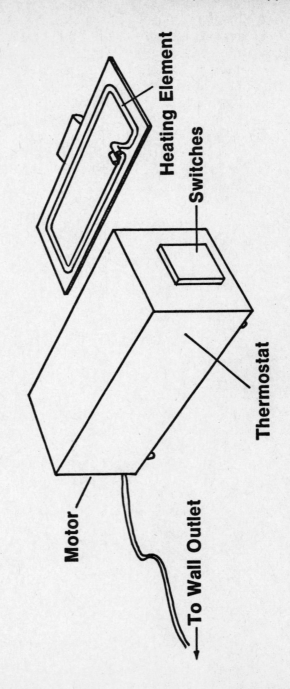

Electric Broiler

Heating Element

Switches

Thermostat

Motor

To Wall Outlet

ILLUSTRATION 1-6. *Exploded View of Electric Broiler*

DIAGNOSING THE ELECTRIC BROILER

PROBLEMS

Broiler Does Not Get Hot .... page 53

Temperature Not Steady .... page 55

Shocks Received from Broiler .... page 55

How to Check Wall Outlet

- Unplug broiler.
- Readjust circuit breaker or fuse.
- Plug in appliance that is known to operate properly.
- If fuse continues to blow, check amp rating of other appliances operating on same power line.
- Total amps per wall outlet should not be more than 15 amps for most home outlets.
- If necessary, turn off appliances until appropriate total amp rate is reached.

How to Check Heating Element

- Unplug broiler.
- Disassemble broiler body.
- Preset volt-ohmmeter to RX 1 scale.
- Attach volt-ohmmeter probe to each end of element.
- Volt-ohmmeter should not indicate high ohms. If it does, replace heating element.

How to Check Power Cord

- Unplug broiler.
- Preset volt-ohmmeter to RX 1 scale.
- Disassemble broiler.
- Attach jumper wire to broiler end of power cord. (See Illustration 1-2.)
- Attach volt-ohmmeter probes to power cord prongs.
- Volt-ohmmeter should indicate zero. If not, replace cord.

How to Check Thermostat

- Unplug broiler.
- Disassemble broiler body.
- Turn temperature selector to high position.
- Preset volt-ohmmeter to RX 1 scale.
- Attach volt-ohmmeter probes to thermostat connections.
- Volt-ohmmeter should indicate zero. If not, replace thermostat.

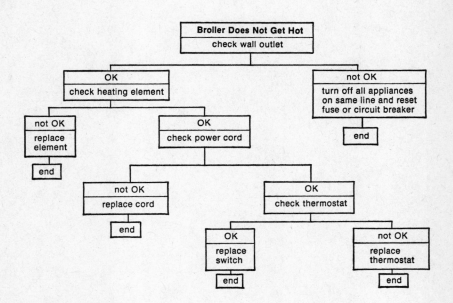

How to Check Temperature Dial

- Unplug broiler.
- Turn temperature dial as far left as possible.
- Dial should indicate "off."
- If not, remove dial and reinstall properly.

How to Check Power Cord

- Unplug broiler.
- Preset volt-ohmmeter to RX 1 scale.
- Disassemble broiler.
- Attach jumper wire to broiler end of power cord.
- Attach volt-ohmmeter probes to power cord probes.
- Volt-ohmmeter should indicate zero. If not, replace cord.

How to Check for Short Circuit

- Unplug broiler.
- Turn temperature selector to high position.
- Preset volt-ohmmeter to RX 1 scale.
- Attach one volt-ohmmeter probe to metal part of broiler.
- Attach second volt-ohmmeter to power cord prong.
- Volt-ohmmeter should indicate low ohms. If not, take unit to professional repair person or replace unit.

How to Check for Grounded Wire

- Unplug broiler.
- Disassemble broiler body.
- Examine all wire connections and look for burn marks.
- Repair broken wire.
- Reassemble.

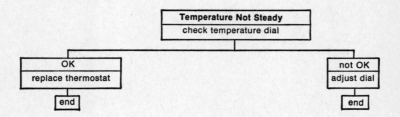

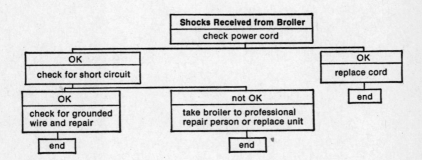

How the Electric Can Opener Works

Every kitchen has a can opener, usually the manual type. With some frustration, the cutting blade separates the top of the can from the rim. Of course, the user has to supply the power, not only to hold the can in place while opening, but also to make the numerous twists of the cutting blade handle. Most of those who frequently use the manual can opener are familiar with the balancing act required to complete the 360 degrees around the edge of the can. Appliance designers have taken the frustration out of opening a can through the development of the electric can opener. (See Illustration 1-7.)

The basic concept of the powered can opener is really not too different from that of the handheld unit. A switch, usually located at the top of the unit, completes the circuit, allowing current to turn the motor. Rotation from the motor shaft is translated to the cutting blade through a series of gears. Compared to the speed of the motor, the opener blade turns slowly, allowing better torque development which is required to cut metal. The reduction in speed is produced by reducing gears. Attached to the motor shaft is a small gear which turns a larger gear connected to the cutting blade. The blade therefore turns proportionately to the revolutions of the opener's motor shaft.

In Summary: The electric can opener uses torque developed through reduced motor rotation to cut metal. (Some can openers have a grindstone. Unlike the cutting blade, torque is not required to sharpen knives and other utensils. The grindstone is directly attached to and powered by the motor.)

Electric Can Opener

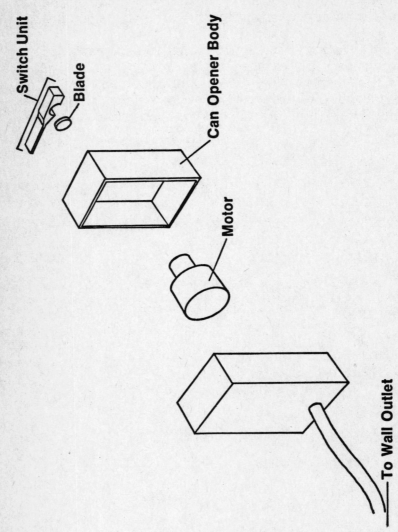

ILLUSTRATION 1-7. *Exploded View of Electric Can Opener*

DIAGNOSING THE ELECTRIC CAN OPENER

PROBLEMS

Can Opener Does Not Operate .... page 61

Can Opener Does Not Cut .... page 63

Can Opener Gives Shocks .... page 65

How to Check Wall Outlet

- Unplug can opener.
- Readjust circuit breaker or fuse.
- Plug in appliance that is known to operate properly.
- If fuse continues to blow, check amp rating of other appliances operating on same power line.
- Total amps per wall outlet should not be more than 15 amps for most home outlets.
- If necessary, turn off appliances until appropriate total amp rate is reached.

How to Check for Jammed Gears

- Plug in can opener.
- Turn on switch.
- If motor does not operate smoothly, gears are jammed.
- Turn off can opener.
- Unplug can opener.
- Disassemble can opener body.
- Check gears and remove obstruction.
- Reassemble.

How to Check Power Cord

- Unplug can opener.
- Preset volt-ohmmeter to RX 1 scale.
- Disassemble can opener gear body.
- Attach jumper wire to both switch terminals.
- Attach volt-ohmmeter probes to power cord prongs. (See Illustration 1-2.)
- Volt-ohmmeter should indicate zero. If not, replace cord.

How to Check Switch

- Unplug can opener.
- Disassemble can opener housing.
- Preset volt-ohmmeter to RX 1 scale.
- Attach volt-ohmmeter probes to switch terminals.
- Turn on switch (can opener still unplugged).
- Volt-ohmmeter should indicate zero. If not, replace switch.

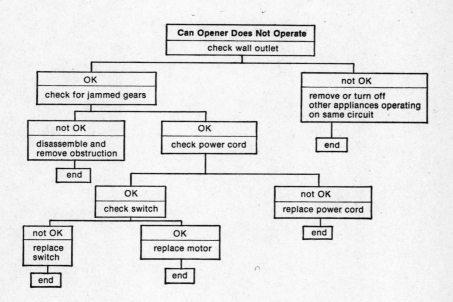

How to Check Cutting Blade

- Plug in can opener.
- Place can in unit.
- Turn on can opener.
- If blades do not cut the can, turn off can opener and remove can.
- Unplug can opener.
- Disassemble can opener body.
- Remove opener blade.
- Examine blade edges.
- If worn, replace.

How to Check Gears

- Plug in can opener.
- Turn on switch.
- If motor does not operate smoothly, gears are obstructed or in poor condition.
- Turn off can opener.
- Unplug can opener.
- Disassemble can opener body.
- Check gears and replace if necessary.
- Reassemble.

How to Check Blade and Gear Connection

- Unplug can opener.
- Disassemble can opener body.
- Examine distance between cutting blade and gear.
- If gear barely touches or does not touch the cutting blade, adjust connection.

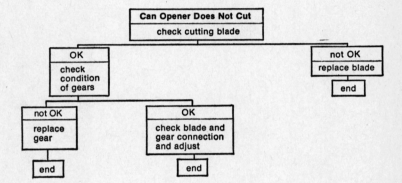

How to Check Power Cord

- Unplug can opener.
- Preset volt-ohmmeter to RX 1 scale.
- Disassemble can opener gear body.
- Attach jumper wire to both switch terminals. (See Illustration 1-2.)
- Attach volt-ohmmeter probes to power cord prongs.
- Volt-ohmmeter should indicate zero. If not, replace cord.

How to Check for Short

- Unplug can opener.
- Preset volt-ohmmeter to RX 100 scale.
- Attach one volt-ohmmeter probe to metal part of can opener.
- Attach other volt-ohmmeter probe to power cord prong.
- Volt-ohmmeter should indicate zero. If not, short exists and appliance should be taken to a professional repair person.

How to Check for Ground Wire

- Unplug can opener.
- Disassemble can opener body.
- Check for poor wire connections.
- Repair defective wire.
- Reassemble.

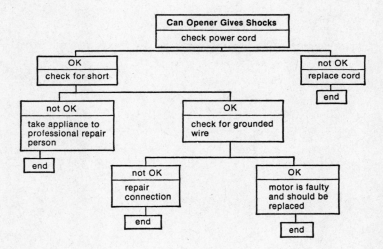

How an Electric Clock Works

Timepieces come in all shapes and varieties. From the expensive seventeen-jewel wristwatch to the simple kitchen clock, all operate in basically the same way and all of them "tell" time. When a timepiece malfunctions, frustrations can set in. An inexpensive clock may be tossed aside and a new one purchased. On the other hand, an expensive clock may be worth the effort involved in locating a watch repair person. In both cases you could probably take care of the situation yourself.

A basic clock has five main parts: the clock case, the motor, the clock movement, the dial, and the crystal. Most problems can be isolated to one of these areas and then the malfunctioned part can be replaced. (See Illustration 1-8.)

Current from the power cord directly enters the clock motor. This differs from other appliances in that there is no switch in the circuit. Through a gear relationship, the motor shaft turns the clock movement assembly. A gear assembly in the clock movement is where time is actually marked. Indicators on the movement shaft point to minutes and hours on the clock dial. On the face of the clock is the crystal, which protects the mechanism from dust and obstructions.

Although most clocks seem to operate indefinitely, proper maintenance should still be kept up to date. Every year, the clock should be disassembled, dust and dirt should be cleaned from the gears, and the gears should be oiled before reassembly.

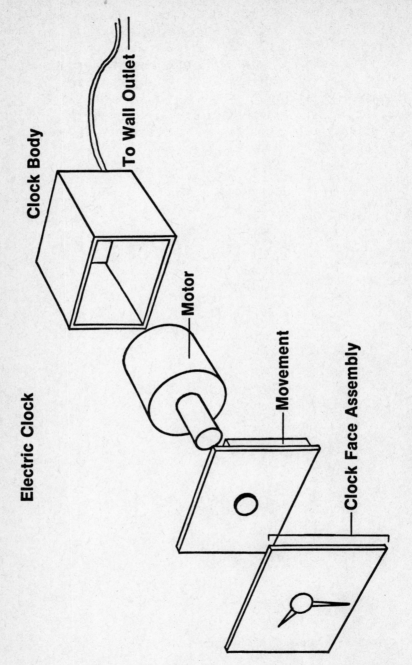

Electric Clock

ILLUSTRATION 1-8. Exploded View of Electric Clock

DIAGNOSING THE ELECTRIC CLOCK

PROBLEMS

Clock Does Not Operate.................... page 71

Noisy Clock................................ page 73

Clock Alarm Not Operating .... page 73

How to Check Wall Outlet

- Unplug clock.
- Readjust circuit breaker or fuse.
- Plug in appliance that is known to operate properly.
- If fuse continues to blow, check amp rating of other appliances operating on same power line.
- Total amps per wall outlet should not be more than 15 amps for most home outlets.
- If necessary, turn off appliances until appropriate total amp rate is reached.

How to Check Power Cord

- Unplug clock.
- Preset volt-ohmmeter to RX 1 scale.
- Disassemble clock.
- Attach jumper wire to clock end of power cord. (See Illustration 1-2.)
- Attach volt-ohmmeter probes to power cord prongs.
- Volt-ohmmeter should indicate zero. If not, replace cord.

How to Check Motor

- Unplug clock.
- Preset volt-ohmmeter to RX 100 scale.
- Disassemble clock.
- Attach volt-ohmmeter probes to clock motor connections.
- If volt-ohmmeter indicates less than 550 or more than 900 ohms, replace motor.

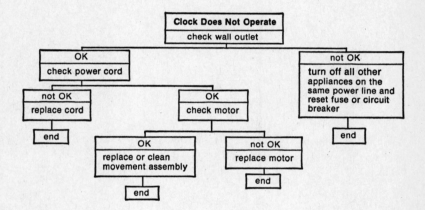

How to Check for Loose Parts

- Unplug clock.
- Disassemble clock.
- Shake parts of the clock and examine for loose parts.
- Tighten loose part.
- Reassemble clock.

How to Check Alarm Button

- Plug in clock.
- Set clock alarm to 12 o'clock.
- Set minute and hour hands to 12 o'clock.
- If alarm does not sound, unplug clock.
- Disassemble clock.
- Check that alarm button contacts are clean. If not, repair contacts.

How to Check Movement Assembly

- Unplug clock.
- Disassemble clock.
- Set clock alarm to 12 o'clock.
- Set minute and hour hands to 12 o'clock.
- Alarm portion of movement assembly should move freely. If not, replace movement assembly.

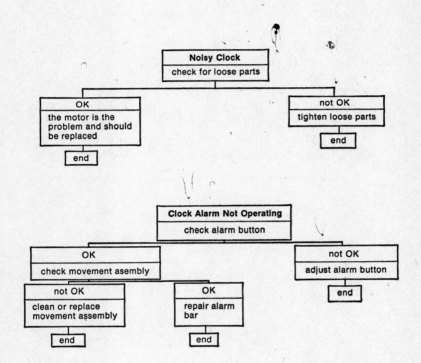

Noisy Clock
check for loose parts

OK
the motor is the problem and should be replaced

end

not OK
tighten loose parts

end

Clock Alarm Not Operating
check alarm button

OK
check movement asembly

not OK
adjust alarm button

end

not OK
clean or replace movement assembly

end

OK
repair alarm bar

end

How Electric Curlers Work

The scene of the lady of the house turning in for the night with a head full of curlers is almost a thing of the past. Curls did not go out of style, but, through the advent of electric hair curlers, the strange "headdress" and uncomfortable sleeping have been eliminated. (See Illustration 1-9.)

In simple terms, wet hair usually remains in the position in which it drys. Hair curlers attached to the hair give shape to each strand of hair. Hair in curlers can dry by two old methods: by natural evaporation of moisture in the air or with the use of a hair dryer. The electric hair curler operates on the same principle as the dryer, except that moisture in the hair evaporates in minutes through direct contact with the curling rod. Electric hair curlers only speed up moisture evaporation to give hair shape in less time.

Current from the power cord directly enters the heating element. This differs from other electric appliances in that an electric hair curler does not contain an on-off switch. Resistance is built up on the heating element due to the small diameter of the element wire. As resistance increases, more and more heat is generated. Most "curling irons," as they are sometimes called, come equipped with a steam system. Water from the steam reservoir, which must be filled before using, will add moisture to the hair as needed.

Electric hair curlers should never by used while near or in water. Hair spray is flammable and should only be used *after* curls have been set with the electric hair curler.

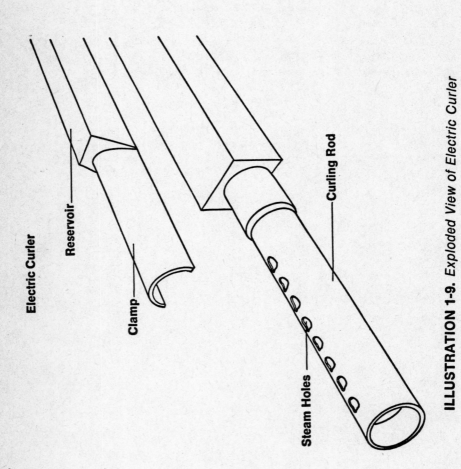

Electric Curler

Reservoir

Clamp

Curling Rod

Steam Holes

ILLUSTRATION 1-9. *Exploded View of Electric Curler*

DIAGNOSING THE HAIR CURLER

PROBLEMS

Hair Curler Does Not Operate............... page 79

Curler Gets Too Hot........................ page 81

Shocks Given by Hair Curler............... page 83

How to Check Wall Outlet

- Unplug hair curler.
- Readjust circuit breaker or fuse.
- Plug in appliance that is known to operate properly.
- If fuse continues to blow, check amp rating of other appliances operating on same power line.
- Total amps per wall outlet should not be more than 15 amps for most home outlets.
- If necessary, turn off appliances until appropriate total amp rate is reached.

How to Check Power Cord

- Unplug hair curler.
- Preset volt-ohmmeter to RX 1 scale.
- Disassemble hair curler body.
- Attach jumper wire to hair curler end of power cord.
- Attach volt-ohmmeter probes to power cord prongs.
- Volt-ohmmeter should indicate zero. If not, replace cord.

How to Check Hair Curler Connection

- Unplug hair curler.
- Disassemble hair curler body.
- Examine hair curler connections for dirty or poor attachment to unit.
- Replace or clean connection and reassemble.

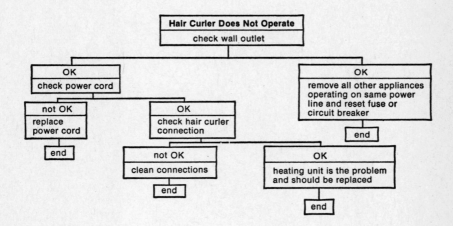

How to Check Steam Vents

- Fill steam reservoir.
- Plug in hair curler.
- Allow hair curler to warm up.
- Depress steam button.
- If steam does not leave the vent holes on the heating element rod, then vents are obstructed.
- Turn off hair curler.
- Let hair curler cool off.
- With a tooth pick, carefully clean each vent hole.

How to Check Hair Curler Connection

- Unplug hair curler.
- Disassemble hair curler body.
- Examine hair curler connections for dirty or poor attachment to unit.
- Replace or clean connection and reassemble.

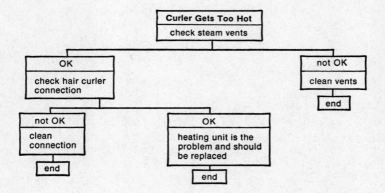

How to Check Power Cord

- Unplug hair curler.
- Preset volt-ohmmeter to RX 1 scale.
- Disassemble hair curler body.
- Attach jumper wire to hair curler end of power cord.
- Attach volt-ohmmeter probes to power cord prongs.
- Volt-ohmmeter should indicate zero. If not, replace cord.

How to Check for Short Circuit

- Unplug hair curler.
- Preset volt-ohmmeter to RX 100 scale.
- Attach one volt-ohmmeter probe to metal part of hair curler.
- Attach second volt-ohmmeter probe to power cord prong.
- Volt-ohmmeter should indicate zero or low ohms. If not, a short exists and unit should either be taken to a professional repair person or replaced with a new unit.

How to Check for Grounded Wire

- Unplug hair curler.
- Disassemble hair curler body.
- Examine all connections in unit for burn marks or poor contacts.
- Repair damaged wire.

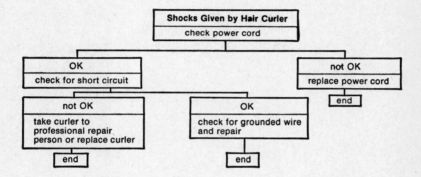

How an Electric Corn Popper Works

Not so many years ago, some families would gather around for a Saturday night at home. In the kitchen the chef for the evening would prepare popcorn. Today on occasion families still pop corn, but they use the electric corn popper instead of the stove. (See Illustration 1-10.)

Corn poppers heat specially dried corn until the kernels explode. The same heat used to pop corn also serves to melt butter, which is automatically distributed to the corn. Heat is generated electrically through the use of a resistance wire called a heating element. Current from the power cord enters the element, where resistance builds, generating heat. If no other devices were installed in the circuit, the heating element would soon burn. To prevent this, manufacturers install a thermostat. Through use of a bimetal contact, the thermostat maintains the preselected temperature. As the current generates heat, the bimetal contact begins to react. When the desired temperature is exceeded, the bimetal contact breaks the circuit, turning the unit off. As the element cools to the selected temperature, the bimetal contact connects the circuit, turning on the corn popper.

There are a few important maintenance notes that should be remembered. Corn poppers cannot be cleaned in dishwashers or in dishpans. The unit must be cleaned with a cloth according to manufacturer's instructions. Corn poppers should be cleaned after every use to prevent buildup of unwanted material.

Electric Corn Popper

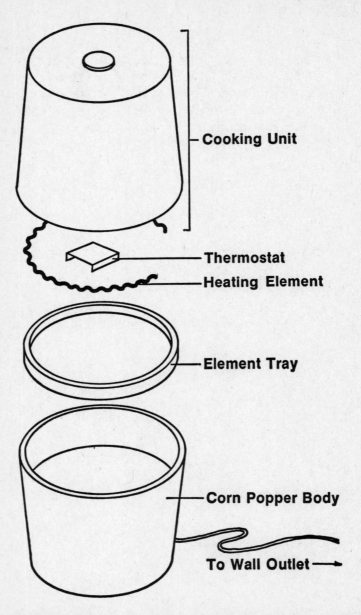

Cooking Unit

Thermostat

Heating Element

Element Tray

Corn Popper Body

To Wall Outlet ⟶

ILLUSTRATION 1-10. *Exploded View of Electric Corn Popper*

DIAGNOSING THE CORN POPPER

PROBLEMS

Corn Popper Does Not Operate .... page 89
Shocks Received from Popper .... page 91

How to Check Wall Outlet

- Unplug corn popper.
- Readjust circuit breaker or fuse.
- Plug in appliance that is known to operate properly.
- If fuse continues to blow, check amp rating of other appliances operating on same power line.
- Total amps per wall outlet should not be more than 15 amps for most home outlets.
- If necessary, turn off appliances until appropriate total amp rate is reached.

How to Check Power Cord

- Unplug corn popper.
- Preset volt-ohmmeter to RX 1 scale.
- Disassemble corn popper.
- Attach jumper wire to corn popper end of power cord. (See Illustration 1-2.)
- Attach volt-ohmmeter probes to power cord prongs.
- Volt-ohmmeter should indicate zero. If not, replace cord.

How to Check Heating Element

- Unplug corn popper.
- Disassemble corn popper body.
- Preset volt-ohmmeter to RX 1 scale.
- Attach volt-ohmmeter to ends of heating element.
- Volt-ohmmeter should indicate zero ohms. If not, replace heating element.

How to Check Thermostat

- Unplug corn popper.
- Disassemble corn popper body.
- Preset volt-ohmmeter to RX 1 scale.
- Attach volt-ohmmeter probes to thermostat connections.
- If volt-ohmmeter indicates high ohms, replace thermostat.

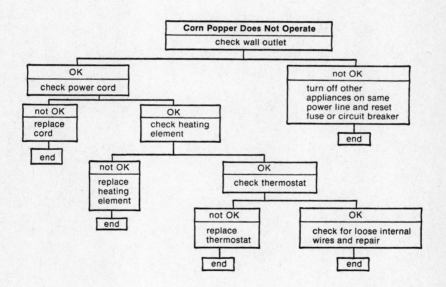

How to Check for Loose Internal Wires

- Unplug corn popper.
- Disassemble corn popper body.
- Examine all wire connections for poor contacts.
- Repair wire.

How to Check for Short Circuits

- Unplug corn popper.
- Preset volt-ohmmeter to RX 100 scale.
- Attach one volt-ohmmeter probe to metal body of corn popper or metal part.
- Attach other volt-ohmmeter probe to power cord prong.
- Volt-ohmmeter should indicate zero. If not, take unit to professional repair person or replace unit.

How to Check for Grounded Wire

- Unplug corn popper.
- Disassemble corn popper body.
- Examine all wire connections for poor contact or burn marks.
- Repair wire.

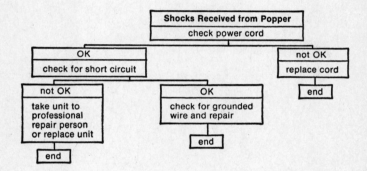

How an Electric Knife Works

Not so long ago, at special family gatherings the dining room table would be set as if for a king. When the traditional turkey or ham was brought out from the kitchen, the head of the family would brandish the long-lived carving knife that had been handed down for generations. However, today, in some families, not only does the family head bring a knife, but also an extension cord. The age of electricity has finally reached the carving platter.

How the electric knife operates is no mystery at all. Power from the wall outlet gives current to the motor in the knife housing. As the motor turns, the motor shaft turns a worm gear. This is a screw-like gear with one continuous groove or tooth. When linked with a worm wheel, which is a gear with teeth cut at an angle, motion from the motor (north-to-south direction) is transferred (east-to-west direction). (See Figure 1-11.)

On the worm wheel is a cam. The post or rivet on the cam is inserted into an elongated hole on the blade drive arm. As the cam turns, the drive arm/cam linkage causes the blade to go back and forth in a cutting action. The blades are held in position by a latch stud and spring arrangement.

As with most electrical appliances, the motor is activated by an on-off switch. This breaks and connects the wires between the motor and the power cord. If we were to let the appliance stand as just described, the knife would only operate at one speed—fast.

To permit various speeds to be devised from a single turning motor, two mechanisms can be used. The first which involves changing gears is not used. Most manufacturers slow down the current to the motor; the less current, the slower the motor. Lowering the current is accomplished by inserting a resistor in the power line before the motor.

In some electric knives which offer variable speeds, the resistor is built into the speed selector unit. Therefore, when low speed is selected there is greater resistance to the current, while for high speed the resistance is low.

In Summary: The electric knife operates by a motor turning a gear arrangement that transfers the direction of power. Through the use of a cam linkage, the cutting action is delivered to the blades.

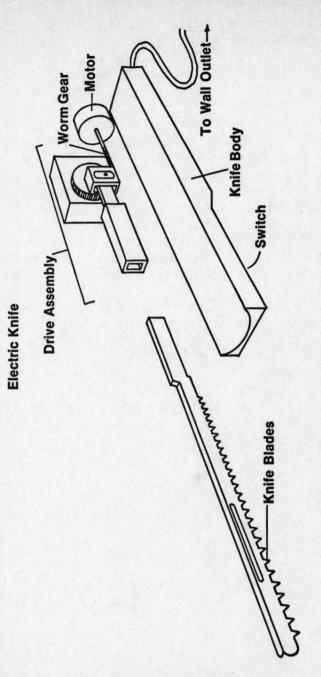

Electric Knife

ILLUSTRATION 1-11. *Exploded View of Electric Knife*

DIAGNOSING THE ELECTRIC KNIFE

PROBLEMS

Knife Does Not Operate .... page 97

Blades Do Not Cut .... page 101

Knife Is Noisy .... page 103

How to Check Wall Outlet

- Unplug knife.
- Readjust circuit breaker or fuse.
- Plug in appliance that is known to operate properly.
- If fuse continues to blow, check amp rating of other appliances operating on same power line.
- Total amps per wall outlet should not be more than 15 amps for most home outlets.
- If necessary, turn off appliances to appropriate total amp rate.

How to Check Power Cord (attached to knife)

- Unplug knife.
- Preset volt-ohmmeter to RX 1 scale.
- Remove knife housing.
- Attach jump wire to power cord inside knife. (See Illustration 1-12.)
- Attach volt-ohmmeter probes to prongs of the power cord.
- OK if meter indicates zero.
- Replace cord if meter does not indicate zero.

How to Check Power Cord (not attached to knife)

- Unplug knife.
- Preset volt-ohmmeter to RX 1 scale.
- Remove plug from knife.
- Attach jump wire to knife end of cord. (See Illustration 1-12.)
- Attach volt-ohmmeter probes to power cord prongs.
- Volt-ohmmeter should indicate zero. If not, replace cord.

How to Check the Switch

- Unplug knife.
- Remove knife housing.
- Preset volt-ohmmeter to RX 1 scale.
- Attach volt-ohmmeter probes to switch wires. (See Illustration 1-13.)
- Switch on knife.
- Volt-ohmmeter should indicate zero. If not, clean or replace switch.

How to Check Drive Unit

- Unplug power cord.
- Remove knife housing.
- Turn fan blade by hand.
- If fan is difficult to turn, remove drive unit and clean.
- Grease worm screw and wheel when reassembling.
- Oil the bearings and reassemble housing.

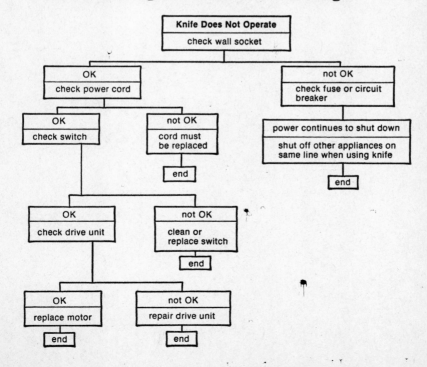

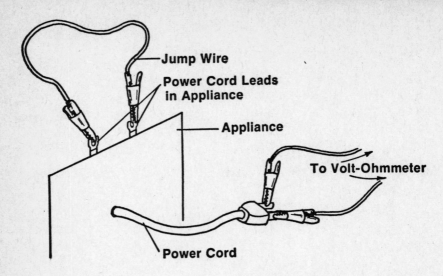

ILLUSTRATION 1-12. *Checking Power Cord Attached to Appliance .*

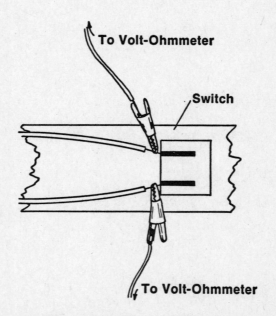

ILLUSTRATION 1-13. *Checking a Switch*

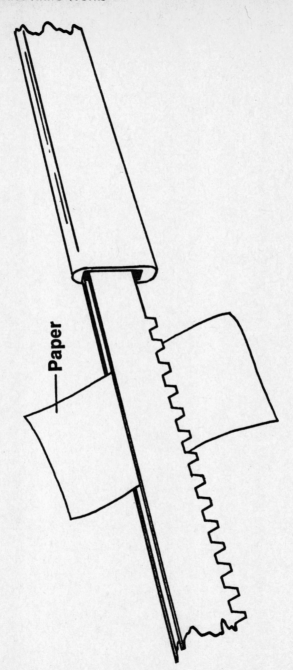

Paper

ILLUSTRATION 1-14. *Checking the Blade Spacing in an Electric Knife*

How to Check for Worn Blades

- Unplug knife.
- Insert blades.
- Check that blades are level with each other and have the same configuration.

How to Check for Blade Spacing

- Unplug knife.
- Insert blades.
- Slip a piece of paper between the blades. (See Illustration 1-14.)
- If paper moves too freely, space is too great. Replace blades.

How to Check Latch Connection

- Plug in knife.
- Insert blades.
- Turn on knife.
- If latch connection moves without blade movement, latch connection is faulty.
- Turn off knife.
- Remove blades.
- Check studs.
- Studs OK if not rounded or marked. If not, replace studs.
- If studs OK, replace latch springs.

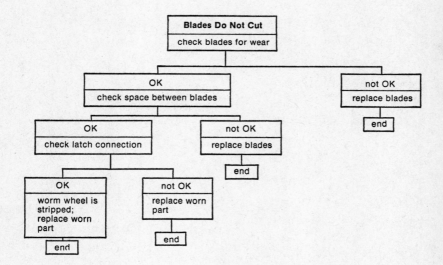

How to Check the Blade Unit

- Plug in knife.
- Insert blades.
- Turn on knife.
- Turn off knife.
- Remove blades.
- Turn on knife.
- If there is no noise when blades are removed, latch connection is faulty.

How to Check Drive Connection

- Unplug knife.
- Remove drive unit.
- Replace drive arms or drive unit, depending upon model of knife.

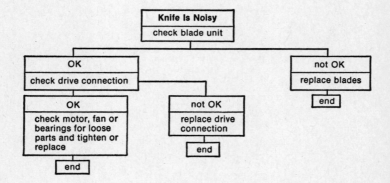

How Electric Shavers Work

Removal of beard stubble is accomplished by several common methods. The traditional method is a sharp piece of metal, a razor blade. As the razor passes the beard stubble, the blade cuts the hair. Whether a manual or electric razor is used, the same basic concept is at work.

When discussing electric shavers, it is important to understand the two basic types, the vibrator head and rotary head, because they are quite different. Blades in the vibrator shaver, easily identified by a relatively flat head, cut using vibrating motion. (See Illustration 1-15.) The rotary shaver blades are driven through gear action.

In the vibrator shaver, current from the power cord enters a magnet assembly. On top of this assembly is the vibrator assembly. As the magnet assembly alters the polarity of the magnet, a vibrator arm with a center pivot is attracted to the polarized side of the magnet. As the speed of changing polarity increases, so does the amount of vibration. Through a linkage, vibrator forks cause the blades to be vibrated at the speed of the vibrator assembly.

In the rotary shaver, current from the power cord enters the shaver motor. Through a gear relationship, the blades are driven directly from the motor shaft.

Both types of shavers should be disassembled each year, cleaned, and all moving parts lubricated. As with all electric appliances, never use an electric shaver with water.

Electric Shaver

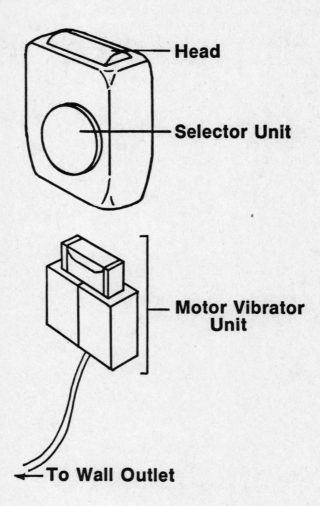

Head

Selector Unit

Motor Vibrator Unit

To Wall Outlet

ILLUSTRATION 1-15. *Exploded View of Electric Shaver (Vibrator Type)*

DIAGNOSING THE ELECTRIC SHAVER

PROBLEMS

Shaver Does Not Operate.................... page 109
Shaver Is Noisy .... page 111

How to Check Wall Outlet

- Unplug shaver.
- Readjust circuit breaker or fuse.
- Plug in appliance that is known to operate properly.
- If fuse continues to blow, check amp rating of other appliances operating on same power line.
- Total amps per wall outlet should not be more than 15 amps for most home outlets.
- If necessary, turn off appliances until appropriate total amp rate is reached.

How to Check Power Cord

- Unplug shaver.
- Preset volt-ohmmeter to RX 1 scale.
- Remove plug from shaver side of power cord.
- Attach jumper wire to shaver end of power cord. (See Illustration 1-2.)
- Attach volt-ohmmeter probes to power cord prongs.
- Volt-ohmmeter should indicate zero. If not, replace cord.

How to Check Switch

- Unplug shaver.
- Preset volt-ohmmeter to RX 1 scale.
- Disassemble shaver.
- Turn switch on.
- Attach volt-ohmmeter probes to each contact of switch.
- Volt-ohmmeter should indicate low or zero ohms. If not, replace switch.

How to Check for Obstruction

- Unplug shaver.
- Disassemble shaver body.
- Examine all internal parts for obstruction.
- Remove obstruction.
- Reassemble.

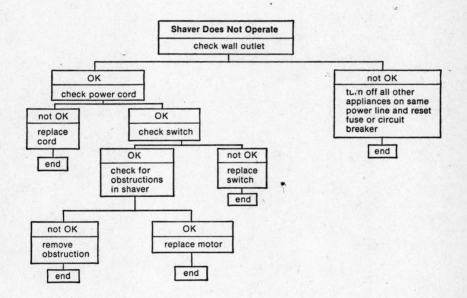

How to Check Blades

- Unplug shaver.
- Disassemble shaver body.
- Examine condition of blades.
- If necessary, replace blades.

How to Check Drive System

- Unplug shaver.
- Disassemble shaver body.
- Examine drive system and manually move internal shaver parts.
- Repair drive system or replace shaver.

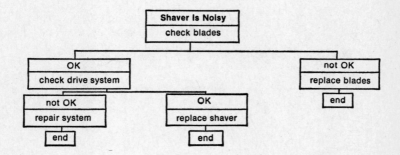

How the Electric Toothbrush Works

The age of motors and electronics has finally broken through to our oral health habits. The electric toothbrush, while still maintaining the traditional toothbrush-like appearance, enables the user to add no other movement than to hold the electric brush in position. (See Illustration 1-16.)

There are two types of electric toothbrushes available in the marketplace. They differ only in that some units are cordless and are sold with a battery charger. Both units with and without a power cord operate in the same manner. Current from the power cord enters either the electric toothbrush directly or into a battery charger. Current powers the brush motor. As the motor shaft rotates, a special gear linkage translates the rotary motion of the shaft to a half-turn motion of the brush shaft.

In the cordless unit, power is generated directly from the battery. When the unit is placed in the electric toothbrush holder, which is the charging unit, the battery regains energy. The charger is linked to the wall outlet and transforms voltage from the house to voltage of the battery (usually from 110 to 9 volts). Voltage is not the only item that must be altered to use the battery-powered brush. Household current is alternating current (AC), while battery current is direct current (DC). A diode in line with the charger transforms AC to DC.

An electric toothbrush is unlike other appliances in that moving parts need not be lubricated. The unit is usually sealed at the factory and disassembly is never required.

Electric
Toothbrush

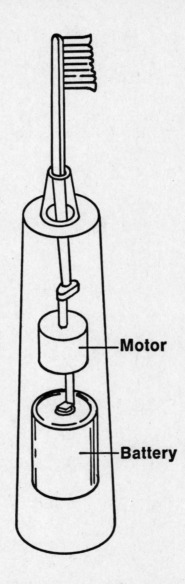

—Motor

—Battery

ILLUSTRATION 1-16. *Exploded View of Electric Toothbrush*

DIAGNOSING THE ELECTRIC TOOTHBRUSH

PROBLEMS

Toothbrush Does Not Operate................ page 117

How to Check Wall Outlet

- Unplug electric toothbrush.
- Readjust circuit breaker or fuse.
- Plug in appliance that is known to operate properly.
- If fuse continues to blow, check amp rating of other appliances operating on same power line.
- Total amps per wall outlet should not be more than 15 amps for most home outlets.
- If necessary, turn off appliances until appropriate total amp rate is reached.

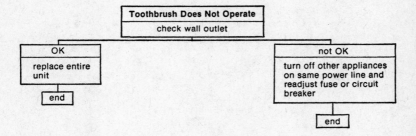

How an Electric Fan
Works

On a hot, windless summer afternoon with 80% humidity, life's frustrations can seem insurmountable. Until your body adapts to the change in climatic conditions, every endeavor requires double the effort it usually demands. Thanks to the invention of the electric fan we can have a selected breeze whenever desired.

When considering the variety of household appliances, the electric fan is one of the simplest units both in function and repair. Power from the wall outlet enters the control unit of the fan, supplying current to rotate the motor. The blade, made from light metal or plastic, is directly connected to the motor shaft. (See Illustration 1-17.) Every turn of the motor shaft will also turn the blade one revolution.

Most electric fans have a speed control unit. Because of the construction of the fan, most units do not use gears to control and modify revolutions per minute of the motor shaft. Instead, speed is controlled electrically through a series of resistors. When the speed selection button is depressed to a low speed, greater resistance is inserted in the power circuit. When a fast speed is desired, the selection unit decreases the resistance in the system, permitting the full draw of current to enter the motor.

Although fans are rather simple, every fan should be cleaned and lubricated each year before the hot season begins. A properly maintained appliance may rarely be in need of repair. Many appliance breakdowns are due to a poor maintenance schedule.

In Summary: Power rotates the motor which causes the fan blades to turn. Resistance in the circuit caused by the speed selection unit enables control of air turbulance from the fan blades.

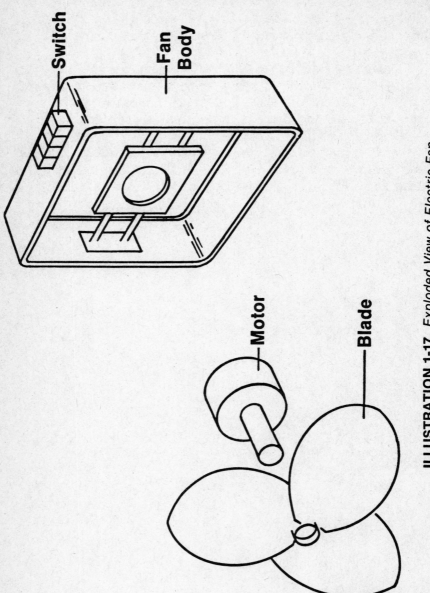

ILLUSTRATION 1-17. *Exploded View of Electric Fan*

DIAGNOSING THE ELECTRIC FAN

PROBLEMS

Fan Does Not Operate...................... page 123

All Speeds Do Not Operate .... page 123

Fan Is Noisy .... page 125

Shocks Felt When Using Fan .... page 127

How to Check Wall Outlet

- Unplug electric fan.
- Readjust circuit breaker or fuse.
- Plug in appliance that is known to operate properly.
- If fuse continues to blow, check amp rating of other appliances operating on same power line.
- Total amps per wall outlet should not be more than 15 amps for most home outlets.
- If necessary, turn off appliances until appropriate total amp rate is reached.

How to Check Power Cord

- Unplug electric fan.
- Preset volt-ohmmeter to RX 1 scale.
- Disassemble fan body.
- Attach jumper wire to switch connection. (See Illustration 1-12.)
- Attach volt-ohmmeter probes to power cord prongs.
- Volt-ohmmeter should indicate zero. If not, replace cord.

How to Check Switch

- Unplug power cord.
- Disassemble fan body.
- Preset volt-ohmmeter to RX 1 scale.
- Attach each volt-ohmmeter probe to terminals of switch.
- Turn on fan (still unplugged).
- Volt-ohmmeter should indicate zero. If not, replace switch.

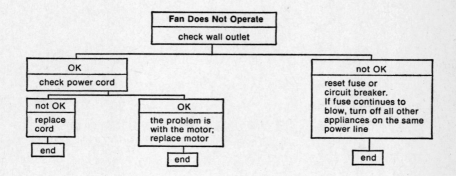

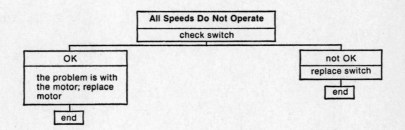

How to Check for Loose Parts

- Plug in fan.
- Turn on fan.
- Listen to various areas of the fan to determine where the loose part is located.
- If necessary, carefully press or hold the suspected part.
- Tighten loose part.

How to Check Fan Blades

- Unplug fan.
- Insert stick or cardboard so that it touches the upper part of the fan blade.
- With the stick or cardboard in place, rotate the fan blade.
- If other blades are bent or unaligned, the stick or cardboard will move markedly.
- Replace fan blade if marked movement is detected.

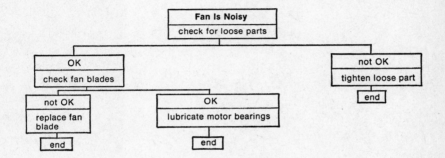

How to Check Power Cord

- Unplug electric fan.
- Preset volt-ohmmeter to RX 1 scale.
- Disassemble fan body.
- Attach jumper wire to switch terminals (See Illustration 1-12.)
- Attach volt-ohmmeter probes to power cord prongs.
- Volt-ohmmeter should indicate zero. If not, replace cord.

How to Check for Short

- Unplug fan.
- Preset volt-ohmmeter to RX 100 scale.
- Attach one volt-ohmmeter probe to metal part of fan.
- Attach other volt-ohmmeter probe to power cord prong.
- Turn on electric fan (still unplugged).
- Volt-ohmmeter should indicate low or zero ohms. If a high ohm indication exists, take fan to professional repair person.

How to Check for Grounded Internal Wire

- Unplug fan.
- Disassemble fan body.
- Examine all wires and wire connections for poor condition.
- Repair wire.
- Reassemble.

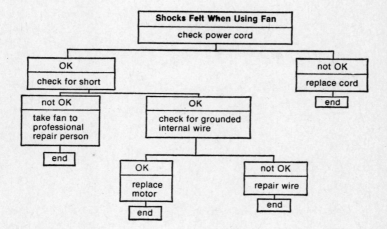

How Handheld Hair Dryers Work

Handheld hair dryers, sometimes called "stylers," come in two basic models: the pro type, which is in the shape of a gun, and the styler, which appears similar to a comb. Although they differ in shape, both handheld dryers operate in the same way. (See Illustration 1-18.)

Current from the power cord enters the dryer switch and temperature selection unit. In most models, temperature switches add or reduce the amount of resistance in the circuit. The greater the resistance, the higher the temperature. The flow of current is then branched into two directions: to the heating element, where resistance in the form of a small-diameter wire generates heat, and to the dryer motor. Attached to the motor shaft is a fan. If a dryer operated without a cooling system, components would overheat within a short period of time. However, the fan and motor assembly help to dissipate excess heat. The fan also moves the heated air from the heating element through the air tube, speeding up the evaporation of moisture in the hair. Most handheld dryers operate using a DC motor rather than an AC unit. Since power from the wall outlet is AC, a mechanism inside the dryer, called a rectifier, must change the current from AC to DC.

Handheld hair dryers must be maintained and lubricated each year. Dryers should never be used anywhere near water. Use hair spray after the hair dryer is turned off, because it is flammable.

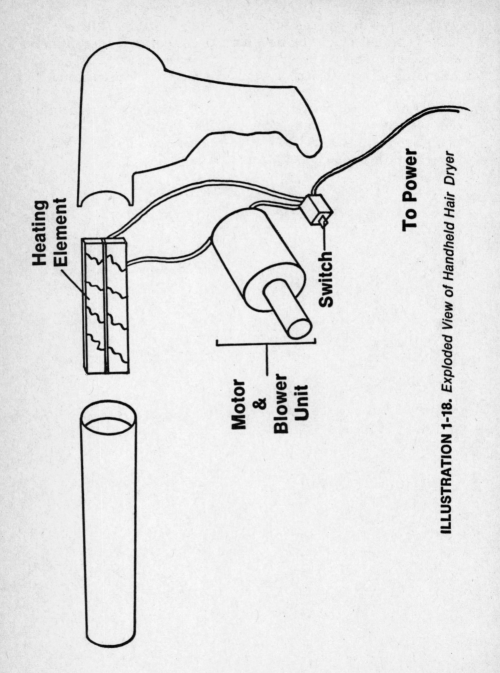

Heating Element

Switch

To Power

Motor & Blower Unit

ILLUSTRATION 1-18. *Exploded View of Handheld Hair Dryer*

DIAGNOSING THE HANDHELD HAIR DRYER

PROBLEMS

Blower Does Not Operate Properly .... page 133
Dryer Does Not Heat .... page 135
Dryer Does Not Operate .... page 135

How to Check Fan Shaft

- Unplug dryer.
- Disassemble dryer body.
- Turn fan manually.
- If fan does not turn properly, examine fan shaft for obstruction.
- Remove obstruction.
- Reassemble fan.

How to Check Heating Element

- Unplug dryer.
- Disassemble dryer body.
- Preset volt-ohmmeter to RX 1 scale.
- Attach each volt-ohmmeter probe to each heating element.
- If volt-ohmmeter indicates high ohms, replace heating element and unit.

How to Check Motor

- Unplug dryer.
- Disassemble dryer body.
- Preset volt-ohmmeter to RX 1 scale.
- Connect each volt-ohmmeter probe to each motor connection.
- If volt-ohmmeter indicates high ohms, replace motor.

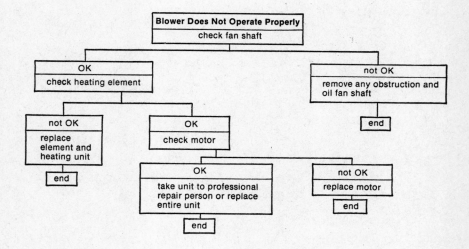

How to Check Switch

- Unplug dryer.
- Disassemble dryer body.
- Examine switch contacts.
- Clean or replace switch if necessary.

How to Check Wall Outlet

- Unplug dryer.
- Readjust circuit breaker or fuse.
- Plug in appliance that is known to operate properly.
- If fuse continues to blow, check amp rating of other appliances operating on same power line.
- Total amps per wall outlet should not be more than 15 amps for most home outlets.
- If necessary, turn off appliances until appropriate total amp rate is reached.

How to Check Power Cord

- Unplug dryer.
- Preset volt-ohmmeter to RX 1 scale.
- Disassemble dryer body.
- Attach jumper wire to dryer end of power cord. (See Illustration 1-2.)
- Attach volt-ohmmeter probes to power cord prongs.
- Volt-ohmmeter should indicate zero. If not, replace cord.

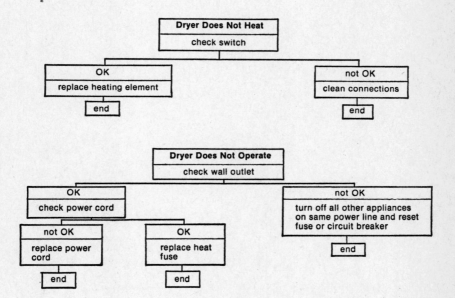

How Heating Pads Work

Muscle spasms and other such ailments can cause discomfort that is usually treated, in part, by supplying heat to the troubled area. Heat is generated basically in two ways: through a chemical substance or a heating pad. The heating pad is similar to the electric blanket except that it concentrates heat rather than disperses heat over the entire area of the bed. (See Illustration 1-19.)

Current from the power cord enters a control center where temperature selection is made and regulated. Temperature is usually controlled in two ways, depending upon the make of the heating pad. Some pads contain a thermostat adjustment. As heat from the blanket reaches the selected temperature, the thermostat, using a bimetal contact, will turn off the pad. When the contact cools, the thermostat will turn the pad on again. Other pads use a resistance control mechanism where each selection button activates a different resistance to the current. The greater the resistance, the hotter the pad will get.

Regardless of the type of temperature control units, heat is generated by resistance in thin wires contained in the heating pad. If current remains the same, the rule-of-thumb states that the thinner the wire, the greater the resistance. As indicated before, a high resistance will generate heat.

Heating pads should never be used on a child or by sleeping individuals because burns can develop quickly. Be sure the heating pad is moisture proof, as such construction, if properly maintained, will give added protection.

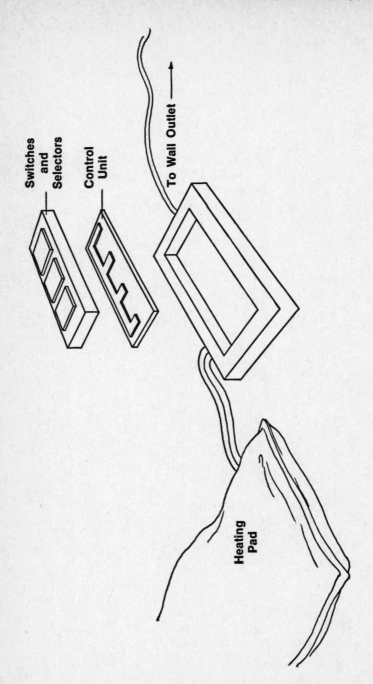

Switches and Selectors

Control Unit

To Wall Outlet →

Heating Pad

ILLUSTRATION 1-19. *Exploded View of Heating Pad*

DIAGNOSING THE HEATING PAD

PROBLEMS

Heating Pad Does Not Operate .... page 141
Heating Pad Is Too Hot .... page 141

How to Check Wall Outlet

- Unplug heating pad.
- Readjust circuit breaker or fuse.
- Plug in appliance that is known to operate properly.
- If fuse continues to blow, check amp rating of other appliances operating on same power line.
- Total amps per wall outlet should not be more than 15 amps for most home outlets.
- If necessary, turn off appliances until appropriate total amp rate is reached.

How to Check On-Off Switch

- Unplug heating pad.
- Disassemble control unit.
- Examine spring operation for each switch.
- If springs do not operate smoothly, adjust or replace switch.
- Examine switch connections. If switch is not making good contact, clean or replace switch.

How to Check Power Cord

- Unplug heating pad.
- Preset volt-ohmmeter to RX 1 scale.
- Disassemble control unit.
- Attach jumper wire to heating pad end of power cord. (See Illustration 1-2.)
- Attach volt-ohmmeter probes to power cord prongs.
- Volt-ohmmeter should indicate zero. If not, replace cord.

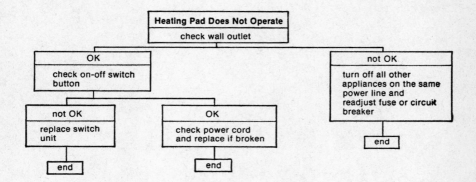

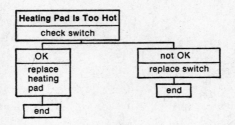

How Hot Plates Work

The conservation of natural gas has revived interest in the use of hot plates to warm soup, tea, and other foods. Experts claim that, unless other foods are prepared at the same time soup or tea is brewing on the stove, there is a waste of natural gas. Hot plates not only conserve natural resources but are convenient to use. With care, a hot plate can be used almost anywhere an outlet exists. (See Illustration 1-20.)

The hot plate operates similar to electric heaters and electric stoves. Current from the power cord follows the circuit through the on-off switch and thermostat and finds resistance in the heating element. This resistance generates enough heat to boil water and brew soup. Adjustments are made to the thermostat to control and maintain the selected temperature. A bimetal contact in the thermostat is heated indirectly by the heating element. When the temperature of the heating element increases beyond the selected setting, the bimetal contact breaks the circuit, turning off the hot plate. As soon as the temperature cools below the desired temperature, the bimetal contact completes the circuit again.

When using a hot plate, make sure that the unit is on a flat surface. Even the slightest unevenness could cause hot liquid to spill. To prevent fires, all food spilled on the hot plate should be cleaned up after every use.

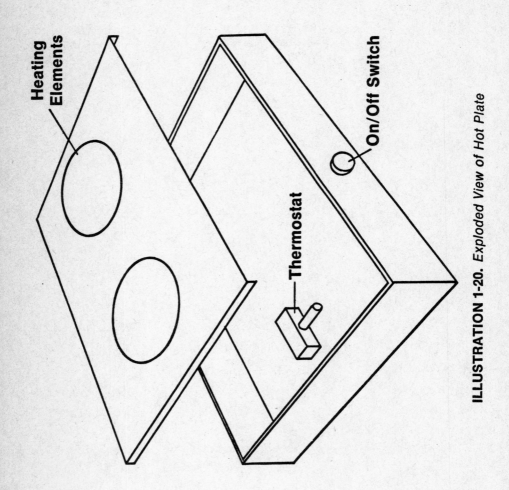

Heating Elements

Thermostat

On/Off Switch

ILLUSTRATION 1-20. *Exploded View of Hot Plate*

DIAGNOSING THE HOT PLATE

PROBLEMS

Hot Plate Does Not Operate .... page 147

Hot Plate Is Too Hot or Too Cold .... page 149

Shocks Received from Hot Plate .... page 149

How to Check Wall Outlet

- Unplug hot plate.
- Readjust circuit breaker or fuse.
- Plug in appliance that is known to operate properly.
- If fuse continues to blow, check amp rating of other appliances operating on same power line.
- Total amps per wall outlet should not be more than 15 amps for most home outlets.
- If necessary, turn off appliances until appropriate total amp rate is reached.

How to Check Power Cord

- Unplug hot plate.
- Preset volt-ohmmeter to RX 1 scale.
- Disassemble hot plate.
- Attach jumper wire to hot plate end of power cord. (See Illustration 1-2.)
- Attach volt-ohmmeter probes to power cord prongs.
- Volt-ohmmeter should indicate zero. If not, replace cord.

How to Check Heating Element

- Unplug hot plate.
- Disassemble hot plate.
- Preset volt-ohmmeter to RX 1 scale.
- Attach volt-ohmmeter probes to each end of the heating element.
- Volt-ohmmeter must not indicate high ohms. If high ohms indicated, replace heating element.

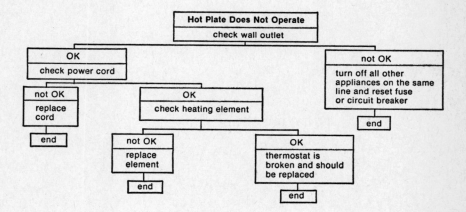

How to Check Control Dial

- Unplug hot plate.
- Turn control dial as far left as possible.
- If dial does not indicate "off," control dial is out of adjustment.
- With dial turned as far left as possible, remove control dial knob.
- Reinstall knob with "off" indicator in proper position.

How to Check Power Cord

- Unplug hot plate.
- Preset volt-ohmmeter to RX 1 scale.
- Disassemble hot plate.
- Attach jumper wire to hot plate end of power cord.
- Attach volt-ohmmeter probes to power cord prongs.
- Volt-ohmmeter should indicate zero. If not, replace cord.

How to Check for Short Circuit

- Unplug hot plate.
- Set control knobs to high position.
- Preset volt-ohmmeter to RX 100 scale.
- Attach one volt-ohmmeter probe to metal part of hot plate.
- Attach other volt-ohmmeter probe to power cord prong.
- Volt-ohmmeter should indicate zero. If not, take hot plate to professional repair person or replace unit.

How to Check for Grounded Wire

- Unplug hot plate.
- Disassemble hot plate.
- Examine all wires and wire connections for poor contacts and burn marks.
- Repair damaged wire.

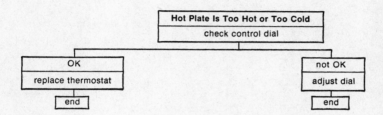

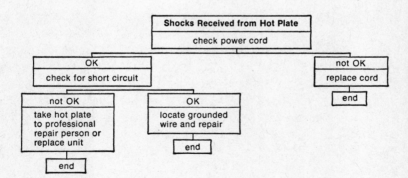

How the Electric Iron Works

With the invention of the heating coil, the iron became a simple device to develop and operate. The mechanism of the electric iron is rather simple. Electricity in the form of current moves through a wire. When we connect both ends of a wire, completing a circuit, the current flows evenly without any obstruction. (See Illustration 1-21.)

However, when we insert a substance that "resists" this flow, the current has greater difficulty in passing through the circuit. This is called resistance to the current. The more resistance in a circuit, the harder the current tries to pass through the material. This causes heat to be given off; the greater the resistance, the greater the amount of heat.

In the base plate of the iron, also called the soleplate, is a wire called the heating element. This transfers heat from the current to the base plate, and from there to the clothes.

The path from the power cord (at the iron end) to the base plate heating element is short, but the current is affected by two primary elements that are built into every iron. Electricity enters the temperature selection unit. This unit is the resistor discussed previously. The hotter the selection, the greater the resistance in the circuit. Although the temperature selection unit determines the relative temperature of the iron, the exact temperature may fluctuate to undesirable limits, making the iron too hot or cold at the wrong time.

To control such an operation, the current, after passing through the temperature control unit, enters the thermostat. Through a bimetal process, the thermostat determines whether the temperature is too hot or too cold and then makes the necessary adjustments.

In Summary: The operation of the iron is, as you can see, rather simple. Electricity flows from the power cord through the temperature control unit, which gives resistance to the current, through the thermostat, which controls the temperature, and then to the heating element in the base plate.

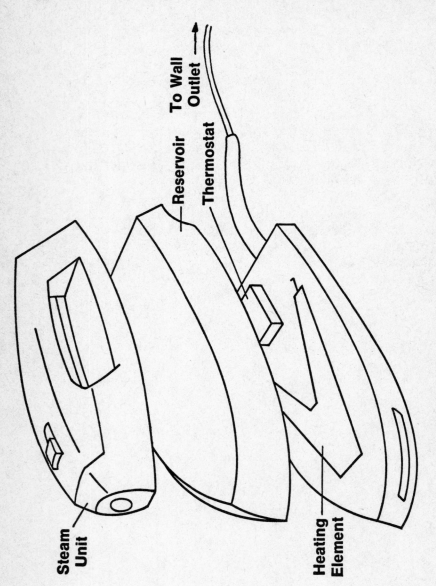

Steam Unit

Reservoir   To Wall Outlet

Thermostat

Heating Element

ILLUSTRATION 1-21. *Exploded View of Electric Iron*

DIAGNOSING THE ELECTRIC IRON

PROBLEMS

Iron Does Not Heat.......................... page 155

Iron Gets Too Hot or Too Cold .... page 157

Iron Slides Too Rough .... page 157

Iron Leaks .... page 159

Steam or Spray Does Not Operate........... page 159

Iron Gives Shocks.......................... page 161

Iron Causes Fuse to Blow .... page 163

How to Check Wall Outlet

- Unplug iron.
- Readjust circuit breaker or fuse.
- Plug in appliance that is known to operate properly.
- If fuse continues to blow, check amp rating of other appliances operating on same power line.
- Total amps per wall outlet should not be more than 15 amps for most home outlets.
- If necessary, turn off appliances until appropriate total amp rate is reached.

How to Check the Power Cord

- Remove rear cover plate from iron.
- Using a jumper wire connect both wires of the cord. (See Illustration 1-2.)
- Preset volt-ohmmeter to RX 1 scale.
- Connect the volt-ohmmeter lead wires to the prongs of the plug.
- If ohm reading is zero, cord is OK.
- If ohm reading is high, replace cord.
- With wire still connected, bend the center of the iron cord.
- If ohm reading moves from zero to high while cord is bent, replace cord.

How to Check Heating Element

- Remove handle, shell, and water tank.
- Locate heating element terminals.
- Preset volt-ohmmeter to RX 1 scale.
- Using probes, touch both heating element terminals.
- Read ohm scale.

- **If meter shows 1 to 25 ohms, heating element is OK.**
- **If meter shows high ohms, check thermostat operation before replacing the heating element and base plate.**

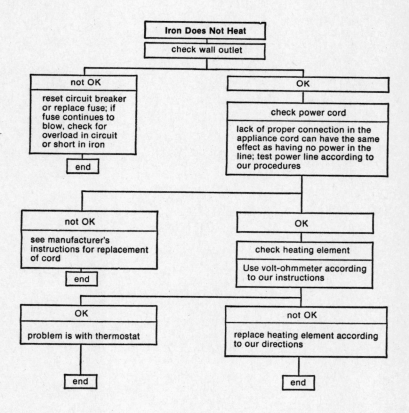

How to Check Thermostat Adjustment

- Remove water from iron.
- Move temperature control to low end of steam selection.
- Hold iron upside down.
- Place thermometer (oven type) on base of iron.
- Plug in and turn on iron.
- Thermometer should read 230°F. to 275°F.
- If thermometer indicates such a temperature, adjustment is OK.
- If not, adjust according to manufacturer's instructions. This usually involves a simple turn of an adjustment screw.

How to Check Thermostat Operation

- Remove handle, shell, and water tank.
- Set volt-ohmmeter to RX 1 scale.
- Read ohm scale.
- Using volt-ohmmeter clips, attach meter to thermostat terminals.
- If meter indicator moves from low to high, thermostat is OK.

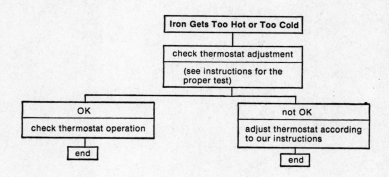

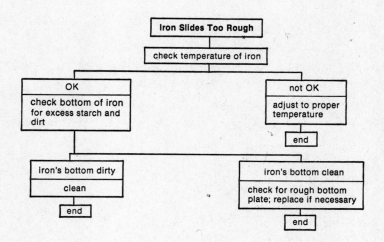

How to Check the Steam Valve

- Remove handle, shell, and water tank.
- Look at valve seat and valve stem pin.
- If broken, replace steam valve.

How to Check Water Tank

- Remove iron cord.
- Remove handle and shell.
- Remove water from tank.
- Fill tank and check for leaks.
- If leaks exist, replace tank and tank gasket.

How to Check Steam Chamber

- Check for cracks in the steam chamber cover.
- If cracks are detected, replace steam chamber cover.
- Check for leaks around the steam chamber seal (between the cover and the iron base).
- If seal leaks, scrape off old sealant.
- Reseal according to sealant manufacturer's instructions.

How to Check Spray Passages

- Spray iron.
- If spray is not operating properly, clean passages.
- With a bent paper clip, pick out dirt from steam holes on bottom of iron.
- Fill iron with vinegar and water in equal parts.
- After 45 seconds plug in iron.
- Place iron on broiler rack and wait until steam stops.
- Let iron operate for another 15 minutes before using.

- Remove steam button and expose spray tube.
- Pick dirt out of tube with needle.
- Reassemble.
- With a fine needle, lightly pick out dirt from the spray nozzle.
- Retest spray.
- If poor spray, replace spray assemblies.

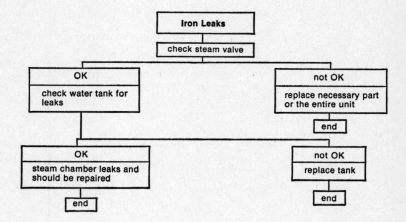

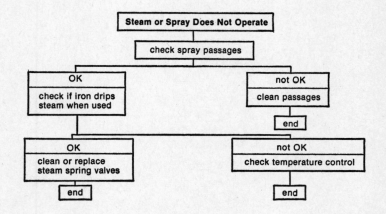

How to Check Power Cord

- Remove rear cover plate from iron.
- Using a jumper wire connect both wires of the cord. (See Illustration 1-2.)
- Preset volt-ohmmeter to RX 1 scale.
- Connect the volt-ohmmeter lead wires to the prongs of the plug.
- If ohm reading is zero, cord is OK.
- If ohm reading is high, replace cord.
- With wire still connected, bend the center of the iron cord.
- If ohm reading moves from zero to high while cord is bent, replace cord.

How to Check for Current Leaks

- Preset volt-ohmmeter to RX 100 scale.
- Place probes onto one prong of plug and the shell of the iron.
- If ohm reading is low, no leak from cord exists.
- If ohm reading is high, leak exists. See professional repair person for proper repair.

How to Check for Grounded Heating Element

- Unplug iron.
- Remove handle, shell, and water tank.
- Turn off temperature control.
- Preset volt-ohmmeter to RX 100 scale.
- Place probe on heating element terminal and base of iron.
- If meter is to right of scale, heating element is grounded.
- Replace heating element.

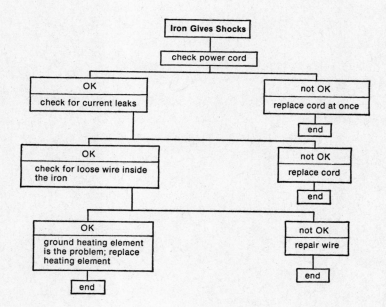

How to Check to See if Circuit Is Overloaded

- Unplug iron.
- Readjust circuit breaker or fuse.
- Plug in appliance that is known to operate properly.
- If fuse continues to blow, check amp rating of other appliances operating on same power line.
- Total amps per wall outlet should not be more than 15 amps for most home outlets.
- If necessary, turn off appliances until appropriate total amp rate is reached.

How to Check for Short Circuit in Iron

- Remove plug.
- Remove handle, shell, water tank, and thermostat.
- While disassembling, check for burn signs, discolored terminals, and poor wire conditions.
- Repair faulty part or contact a repair person.

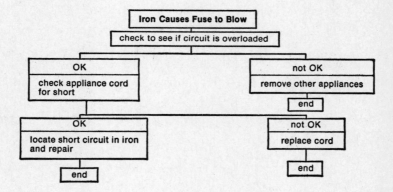

How the Electric Mixer Works

Using manual egg beaters was once a tradition in the kitchen. Since beating thick food became more a chore than a cooking enjoyment, technology took the labor out of beating and devised a motor-driven beater. This beater did not work at only one speed or sensitivity as had the manual egg beater. Adjustments could be made to allow mixing from the thickest pudding to even a light refreshing drink. The electric beater became less a beater and more the common mixer. (See Illustration 1-22.)

The mixer is powered by an electric motor. Current is received from the power cord and translated into rotating motion in the motor. At the end of the motor shaft is a gear assembly that consists of a worm gear, which is directly connected to the motor shaft, and two round gears. The worm gear translates vertical rotational motion from the motor to horizonal rotation of the round gears. The round gears power the beaters through the beater linkage. The beater linkage contains the beater coupling and ejector mechanism, usually a spring.

Similar to other electrical appliances, control of the speed of the mixer is accomplished through resistance to the current. The speed control unit contains several resistors: the greater the resistance, the slower the motor operates; the lower the resistance, the faster the motor operates.

When the mixer operates at slower speeds for a prolonged period of time, heat is generated. Resistance to current flow is one of the major reasons for heat generation. If the appliance operates for long periods without either periodic rest or a cooling system built into the appliance, it would overheat and could burn out the motor or speed control.

To prevent overheating, appliances such as the mixer usually contain a fan. The mixer fan, located on the motor shaft, enables a quicker transfer of heat from the components to the air.

In Summary: Power from the wall outlet causes the motor to turn. Such vertical rotation is translated by the worm gear to horizontal rotation in the round gears. In turn, the round gears through a beater linkage turn the beaters. The speed of the beater is controlled by resistors in the speed control unit.

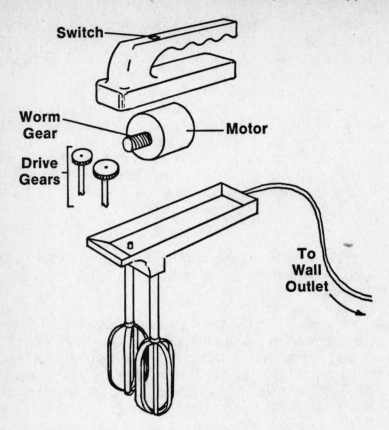

ILLUSTRATION 1-22. *Exploded View of Electric Mixer*

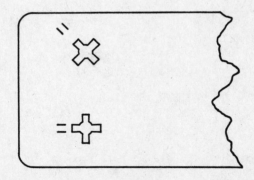

ILLUSTRATION 1-23. *Checking Beater Slots in Electric Mixer*

DIAGNOSING THE ELECTRIC MIXER

PROBLEMS

Mixer Does Not Operate .... page 169

Beaters Do Not Turn .... page 171

Mixer Is Noisy .... page 173

Mixer Gives Shocks .... page 175

How to Check Wall Outlet

- Unplug mixer.
- Readjust circuit breaker or fuse.
- Plug in appliance that is known to operate properly.
- If fuse continues to blow, check amp rating of other appliances operating on same power line.
- Total amps per wall outlet should not be more than 15 amps for most home outlets.
- If necessary, turn off appliances until appropriate total amp rate is reached.

How to Check Power Cord (attached to mixer)

- Unplug mixer.
- Preset volt-ohmmeter to RX 1 scale.
- Remove mixer housing.
- Attach jump wire to power cord inside mixer. (See Illustration 1-12.)
- Attach volt-ohmmeter probes to prongs of power cord.
- OK if meter indicates zero.
- Replace cord if meter does not indicate zero.

How to Check Power Cord (not attached to mixer)

- Unplug mixer.
- Preset volt-ohmmeter to RX 1 scale.
- Remove plug from mixer.
- Attach jumper wire to mixer end of cord. (See Illustration 1-2.)
- Attach volt-ohmmeter probes to power cord prongs.
- Volt-ohmmeter should indicate zero. If not, replace cord.

How to Check Thickness of Food

- Plug in mixer.
- Remove mixer from food.
- Turn on mixer.
- Adjust to all speeds.
- If beaters turn properly, food is too thick. Adjust mixer to higher speed.

How to Check Mixer Switch

- Unplug mixer.
- Remove mixer housing.
- Preset volt-ohmmeter to RX 1 scale.
- Attach volt-ohmmeter probes to switch wire.
- Switch on mixer.
- Volt-ohmmeter should indicate zero. If not, clean or replace switch.

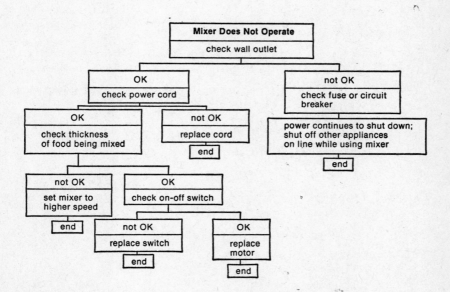

How to Check if Beaters Are Inserted Properly

- Plug in mixer.
- Remove beaters.
- Turn on mixer.
- If operating properly, turn mixer off.
- Unplug mixer.
- Insert beaters (you should hear a "snap" when beaters are locked into position).
- If snap is not heard, gears are clogged.
- Remove beaters.
- Remove mixer body and gears.
- Remove dirt from gears and soak gears in soapy water.
- When dry, replace gears and lubricate.
- Reassemble body.

How to Check if Beaters Clash

- Plug in mixer.
- Remove beaters.
- Compare beater slots to illustration. (See Illustration 1-23.)
- If beater slots differ, beaters are out of alignment.
- Unplug mixer.
- Remove mixer body.
- Remove gear cover.
- Adjust beater and worm gears.
- Reassemble unit.

How to Check for Stripped Beater Gears

- Unplug mixer.
- Insert beater.

- Turn beater by hand.
- If beater turns, gears are stripped.
- Remove mixer body.
- Remove both gears.
- Install new gears.
- Align new gears.
- Reassemble.

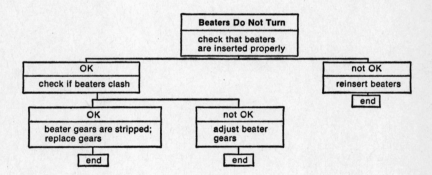

How to Check if Beaters Hit Each Other

- Plug in mixer.
- Insert beater
- Turn on mixer.
- Set mixer to low speed.
- Look to see if beaters are hitting.
- Turn off mixer.
- Check beater shafts to assure straightness. If not straight, replace beaters.
- Remove beaters.
- Beater slots on mixer should be positioned similar to those in the illustration. If not, beaters are out of alignment. (See Illustration 1-23.)
- Unplug mixer.
- Remove mixer body.
- Remove gear cover.
- Adjust beater and worm gears.
- Reassemble unit.

How to Check for Loose Parts

- Plug in mixer
- Turn on mixer.
- Carefully touch various parts of the mixer to find loose parts.
- Turn off mixer.
- Unplug mixer.
- Tighten parts.

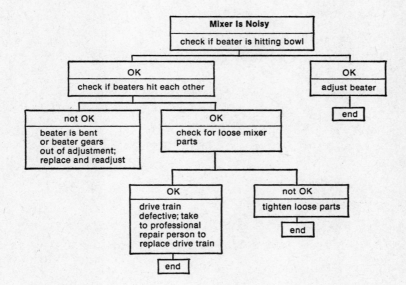

How to Check Power Cord (attached to mixer)

- Unplug mixer.
- Preset volt-ohmmeter to RX 1 scale.
- Remove mixer housing.
- Attach jump wire to power cord inside mixer. (See Illustration 1-12.)
- Attach volt-ohmmeter probes to prongs of power cord.
- OK if meter indicates zero.
- Replace cord if meter does not indicate zero.

How to Check Power Cord (not attached to mixer)

- Unplug mixer.
- Preset volt-ohmmeter to RX 1 scale.
- Remove plug from mixer.
- Attach jumper wire to mixer end of cord. (See Illustration 1-2.)
- Attach volt-ohmmeter probes to power cord prongs.
- Volt-ohmmeter should indicate zero. If not, replace cord.

How to Check for Shocks from Metal Parts of Mixer

- Unplug mixer.
- Preset volt-ohmmeter to RX 100 scale.
- Set mixer speed to high.
- Attach volt-ohmmeter probe to speed control unit.
- Attach second volt-ohmmeter probe to metal part of mixer.
- Volt-ohmmeter should read zero to low ohms if no leak is present. If a high reading is noticed, take mixer to a professional repair person or return it to the manufacturer.

How to Check for Grounded Wire in Mixer

- Unplug mixer.
- Remove mixer body.
- Check inside mixer for bare wires or burn areas.
- If bare wires or burn areas are noticed, replace power cord.

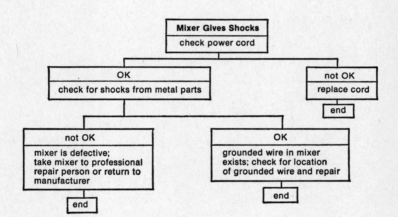

How Space
Heaters Work

In rooms or open areas where central heating units are not available, the most common way of warming the area is by using a space heater. A space heater is also used to supplement existing heating systems. (See Illustration 1-24.)

Current from the power cord enters the unit and separates. The current flow is directed to both the motor and the heating element. As with other appliances, the space heater is equipped with an on-off switch and a temperature selection button or dial. Once turned on, current flows to the motor, which contains a fan attached to the motor shaft. The fan circulates air, serves as a cooling system for the space heater components, and provides air current to circulate heat from the heating elements. Adjustments to the temperature selection button or dial fine-tune the space heater's thermostat, which regulates the temperature of the unit. As resistance from the thin diameter heating elements

causes heat to generate, the thermostat's bimetal
connection reacts. Once the bimetal contact is heated
beyond the predetermined temperature, the unit is turned
off. As soon as the bimetal strip cools to below the cut-off
point, the contacts complete the circuit and turn the space
heater on. To assure that most of the generated heat is
transmitted in the proper direction, most manufacturers
install a reflection shield behind the heating element. The
shield reflects the heat away from the undesirable area.

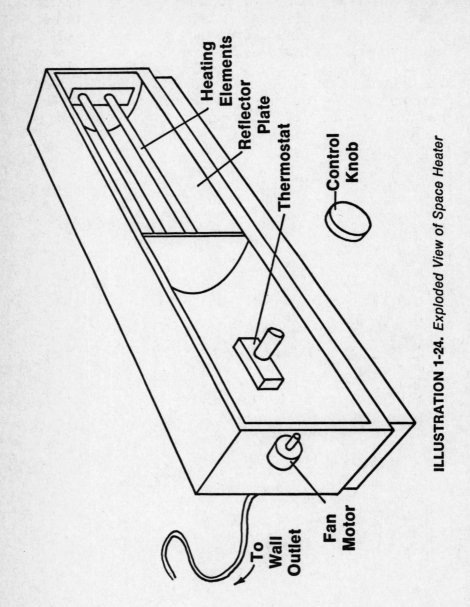

ILLUSTRATION 1-24. *Exploded View of Space Heater*

DIAGNOSING THE SPACE HEATER

PROBLEMS

Space Heater Does Not Operate .... page 181

Motor Does Not Operate.................... page 181

Shocks Given by Heater .... page 183

How to Check Wall Outlet

- Unplug space heater.
- Readjust circuit breaker or fuse.
- Plug in appliance that is known to operate properly.
- If fuse continues to blow, check amp rating of other appliances operating on same power line.
- Total amps per wall outlet should not be more than 15 amps for most home outlets.
- If necessary, turn off appliances until appropriate total amp rate is reached.

How to Check Power Cord

- Unplug space heater.
- Preset volt-ohmmeter to RX 1 scale.
- Disassemble space heater.
- Attach jumper wire to space heater end of power cord. (See Illustration 1-2.)
- Attach volt-ohmmeter probes to power cord prongs.
- Volt-ohmmeter should indicate zero. If not, replace cord.

How to Check Thermostat

- Unplug space heater.
- Disassemble sides of space heater.
- Move thermostat weight with finger. If thermostat weight does not move freely, replace thermostat.

How to Check Motor for Obstruction

- Unplug space heater.
- Turn temperature selector to high.
- Disassemble space heater.
- Turn fan manually.
- If fan does not turn freely, examine motor shaft for obstruction.
- Remove obstruction.
- Reassemble.

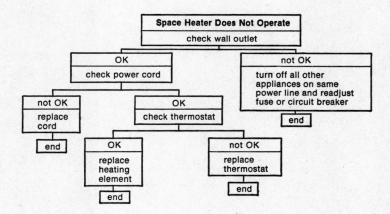

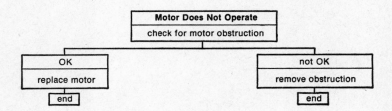

How to Check for Short Circuit

- Unplug space heater.
- Preset volt-ohmmeter to RX 100 scale.
- Set selector to high.
- Attach a volt-ohmmeter probe to a metal part of the space heater.
- Attach the other volt-ohmmeter probe to the power cord prong.
- Volt-ohmmeter should indicate zero or low ohms. If not, take unit to professional repair person or replace entire unit.

How to Check for Grounded Wire

- Unplug space heater
- Disassemble space heater body.
- Examine all wire connections for poor contact or burn marks.
- If poor contact or burn marks, repair wire.

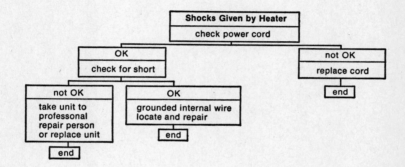

How a Toaster Works

A cup of tea and a slice of toast always seem to be one of the prime homemade remedies for any ailment, second only to the famed chicken soup. Of course, there are times when preparing toast can be even more frustrating than baking a cake for the first time. Either each slice of toast differs too much in color or the bread becomes jammed in the top lip of the toaster. Usually there is a reason for the problem: the toaster is malfunctioning or it is out of adjustment. (See Illustration 1-25.)

Understanding how the toaster operates will lend some insight into the situation and its remedies. As with so many heating appliances, bread is cooked through a transfer of heat from the heating element in the toaster. Current from the power cord is in line with the heating elements. Resistance to the current, caused by the decrease in size of the wires of the heating element compared with the size of the power cord, generates heat. The temperature of the heating wires is hot enough to cook the slice of bread.

The degree to which the bread is cooked is determined by a thermostat. Adjustments to the thermostat enable heat from the heating element to reach a predetermined temperature at which point the toaster will automatically turn off. The thermostat is a bimetal electrical connection. When the bimetal element is heated, the element expands, breaking the connection and causing the toast to pop.

The popping action occurs through a spring-activated piston and a linkage to the thermostat. When the temperature reaches the selected temperature, the thermostat activates the linkage, causing the piston to release and the toast to rise.

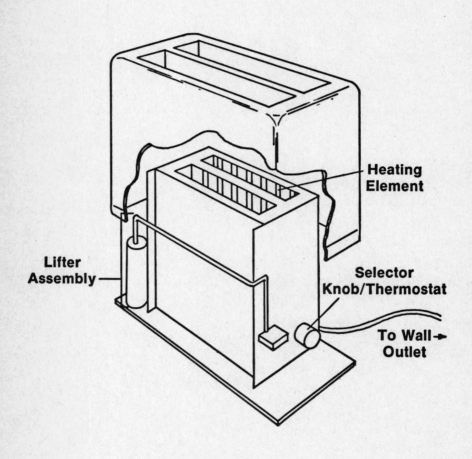

ILLUSTRATION 1-25. *Exploded View of Toaster*

DIAGNOSING THE TOASTER

PROBLEMS

Toast Carrier Does Not Operate............. page 189

Toaster Does Not Operate .... page 189

Toaster Does Not Toast Properly............ page 191

Toaster Burns Toast........................ page 193

Toaster Gives Shocks .... page 195

How to Check for Obstruction of Carrier

- Unplug toaster.
- Depress lift lever.
- If carrier is obstructed, examine both slots.
- Remove obstruction. If necessary, remove bottom of toaster to gain access to obstruction.

How to Check the Release Switch

- Unplug toaster.
- Depress lift lever.
- Lock lift lever.
- Plug in toaster.
- Lift lever should not rise. If lift lever returns to "off" position, release switch should be replaced.

How to Check Wall Outlet

- Unplug toaster.
- Readjust circuit breaker or fuse.
- Plug in appliance that is known to operate properly.
- If fuse continues to blow, check amp rating of other appliances operating on same power line.
- Total amps per wall outlet should not be more than 15 amps for most home outlets.
- If necessary, turn off appliances until appropriate total amp rate is reached.

How to Check Power Cord

- Unplug the toaster.
- Preset volt-ohmmeter to RX 1 scale.
- Disassemble toaster body.
- Attach jumper wire to toaster end of power cord. Illustration 1-2.)

- Attach volt-ohmmeter probes to power cord prongs.
- Volt-ohmmeter should indicate zero. If not, replace cord.

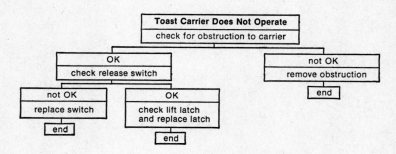

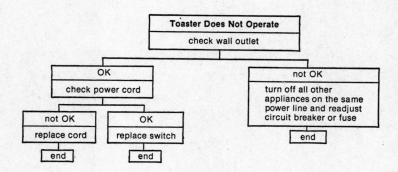

How to Check Thermostat

- Plug in the toaster.
- Place bread in toaster.
- Place selection knob to center position.
- Depress lift lever.
- Toast should be medium brown. If not, replace thermostat.

How to Check for Obstruction in Toaster Body

- Unplug toaster.
- Depress toast carrier until it locks.
- Examine the heating elements of each slot.
- Remove any obstruction found on the heating elements.

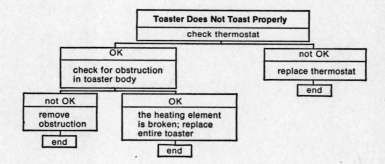

How to Check Heating Elements

- Plug in toaster.
- Insert slice of bread.
- Place selection dial in center.
- Depress lift lever.
- If toast is brown on only one side, heating element is bad and toaster should be replaced.

How to Check the Switch

- Plug in toaster.
- Insert a slice of bread.
- Place selection dial in center.
- Depress lift lever.
- When toaster pops, heating elements should be off. If not, switch is faulty and must be replaced.

How to Check Thermostat

- Plug in toaster.
- Place bread in toaster.
- Place selection knob to center position.
- Depress lift lever.
- Toast should be medium brown. If not, replace thermostat or the entire toaster.

How to Check Lift Spring

- Unplug toaster.
- Depress lift lever and lock it.
- Gently push up on lift lever.
- If lift lever does not rise, replace lift spring.

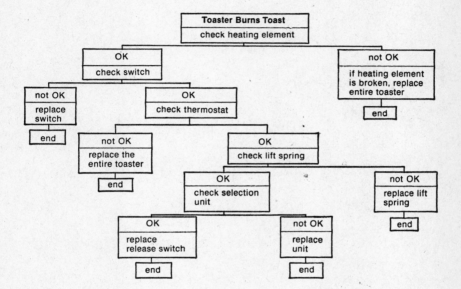

How to Check Power Cord

- Unplug the toaster.
- Preset volt-ohmmeter to RX 1 scale.
- Disassemble toaster body.
- Attach jumper wire to toaster end of power cord. (See Illustration 1-2.)
- Attach volt-ohmmeter probes to power cord prongs.
- Volt-ohmmeter should indicate zero. If not, replace cord.

How to Check for Short

- Unplug toaster.
- Preset volt-ohmmeter to RX 100 scale.
- Depress lift lever and lock.
- Attach one volt-ohmmeter probe to metal part of toaster.
- Attach second volt-ohmmeter probe to power cord prong.
- Volt-ohmmeter should indicate low to zero ohms. If not, take toaster to a professional repair person.

How to Check for Grounded Internal Wire

- Unplug toaster.
- Disassemble toaster body.
- Examine all wires and heating elements for poor condition.
- Repair defective wire.

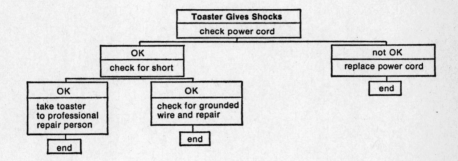

How the Vacuum Cleaner Works

Two types of vacuum cleaners are in use today. They are the floor type, which requires assembly and disassembly of attachments, and the upright model, which is easily stored in closets without the need to add parts in order to operate. (See Illustration 1-26.) Although the units are different in style, both operate on a similar principle: The state of vacuum is really a void—nothing exists in the area where vacuum exists. Before going into detail about the mechanism of a vacuum cleaner, a brief example of vacuum is in order.

In our environment the force of atmospheric pressure around every object keeps the object in general equilibrium. That is, if pressure is removed from one side of the object, the object will fall or move in the direction with the least amount of pressure. Consider a piece of dirt on the floor. Pressure is acting equally on all four sides of the dirt. The vacuum cleaner removes pressure from the other three sides to force the dirt into the vacuum cleaner.

To remove one side of pressure, the vacuum cleaner must create a vacuum. Current from the power cord activates the motor. A specially designed fan is attached to the motor shaft. As the motor rotates, air is forced by the fan from one side of the vacuum hose to the bag end of the vacuum cleaner. Such movement creates increased pressure on the bag end of the vacuum hose and a negative pressure or vacuum on the other side of the vacuum hose. As long as the fan turns, enough vacuum is created to remove pressure from a small object and "lift" the object into the vacuum cleaner bag.

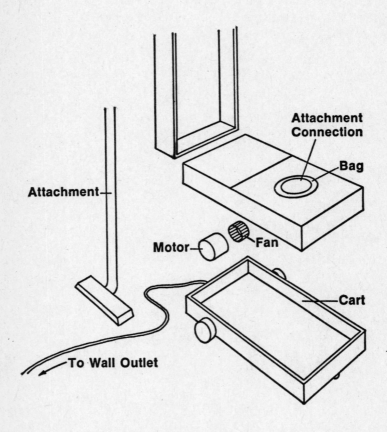

ILLUSTRATION 1-26. *Exploded View of Vacuum Cleaner*

DIAGNOSING THE VACUUM CLEANER

PROBLEMS

Vacuum Cleaner Does Not Operate .... page 201

Vacuum Cleaner Does Not Pick Up Dirt ..... page 203

Cleaner Is Too Noisy .... page 203

Shocks Received from Cleaner.............. page 205

How to Check Wall Outlet

- Unplug vacuum cleaner.
- Readjust circuit breaker or fuse.
- Plug in appliance that is known to operate properly.
- If fuse continues to blow, check amp rating of other appliances operating on same power line.
- Total amps per wall outlet should not be more than 15 amps for most home outlets.
- If necessary, turn off appliances until appropriate total amp rate is reached.

How to Check Power Cord

- Unplug vacuum cleaner.
- Preset volt-ohmmeter to RX 1 scale.
- Disassemble vacuum cleaner body.
- Attach jumper wire to vacuum cleaner end of power cord. (See Illustration 1-2.)
- Attach volt-ohmmeter probes to power cord prongs.
- Volt-ohmmeter should indicate zero. If not, replace cord.

How to Check Fan for Obstruction

- Unplug vacuum cleaner.
- Disassemble vacuum cleaner body.
- Turn fan blade manually.
- Examine for obstruction.
- Remove obstruction.
- Reassemble vacuum cleaner body.

How to Check Switch

- Unplug vacuum cleaner.
- Preset volt-ohmmeter to RX 1 scale.
- Disassemble vacuum cleaner.
- Turn on vacuum cleaner (still unplugged).
- Attach volt-ohmmeter probes to switch connections.
- Volt-ohmmeter should indicate zero. If not, replace switch.

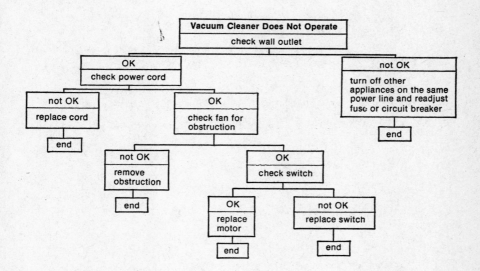

How to Check for Obstruction in Hose

- Unplug vacuum cleaner.
- Examine vacuum hose for obstruction.
- Remove obstruction.
- If obstruction is not found, check bag and empty if necessary.

How to Check for Hose Leaks

- Plug in vacuum cleaner.
- Turn on vacuum cleaner.
- Examine all attachment connections for leaks.
- Repair or replace faulty part.

How to Check Fan

- Unplug vacuum cleaner.
- Disassemble vacuum cleaner body.
- Turn fan manually.
- If fan is obstructed, remove obstruction.
- Examine fan blades and replace fan if damaged.

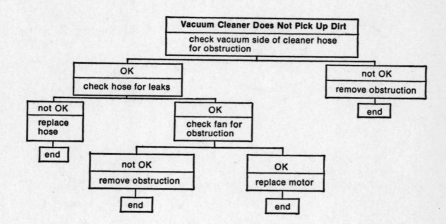

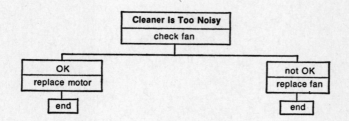

How to Check Power Cord

- Unplug vacuum cleaner.
- Preset volt-ohmmeter to RX 1 scale.
- Disassemble vacuum cleaner body.
- Attach jumper wire to vacuum cleaner end of power cord. (See Illustration 1-2.)
- Attach volt-ohmmeter probes to power cord prongs.
- Volt-ohmmeter should indicate zero. If not, replace cord.

How to Check for Short Circuit

- Unplug vacuum cleaner.
- Preset volt-ohmmeter to RX 1 scale.
- Attach one volt-ohmmeter probe to metal part of vacuum cleaner.
- Attach other volt-ohmmeter probe to power cord prongs.
- Volt-ohmmeter should indicate zero or low ohms. If not, take unit to professional repair person or replace unit.

How to Check for Grounded Wire

- Unplug vacuum cleaner.
- Disassemble vacuum cleaner body.
- Examine all wire connections for poor contacts or burn marks.
- Repair wire.
- Reassemble.

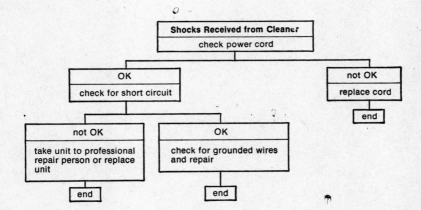

Section II

How to Repair
Large Appliances

Reminder: Always follow proper safety procedures.
(See Appendix A.)

How a Clothes Dryer Works

Not too long ago, backyards were the scene of "flag flying" once or twice a week, in other words, wash day. The line of clothes hanging out to dry could easily be used as opening day banners for a store. Clotheslines have become almost a thing of the past since the onset of the clothes dryer.

Although the world of appliances has eased the chore of drying clothes, the basic principle is the same as if the clothes were still being hung on the line. Air is used to remove the excess moisture in the clothes caused by washing. The hotter the air and the stronger the breeze, the faster the clothes will dry.

In the clothes dryer, air is heated by either a heating element in the electric-powered dryer or a gas jet in the gas dryer. The second component required to dry clothes, the breeze, is supplied by a blower system. An electric motor powers the blower which forces hot air through air ducts into the dryer drum. To be sure the heated air contacts every area of the clothes, the dryer drum rotates, forcing the clothes to toss. The drum is powered by the same motor as the blower. The temperature is monitored by a thermostat, a bimetal contact that, when heated to a desired temperature, breaks the connection. When the contact cools below the selected temperature, the connection is made. Most models also come with an overload system. If the weight of the clothes in the dryer drum is beyond the prescribed limit set by the manufacturer, the unit will not operate.

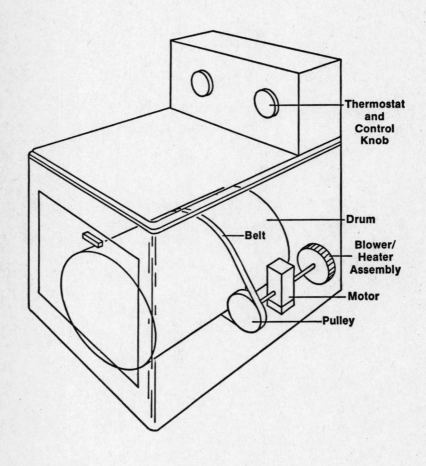

ILLUSTRATION 2-1. *Exploded View of Clothes Dryer*

DIAGNOSING THE CLOTHES DRYER

PROBLEMS

Clothes Dryer Does Not Operate .... page 213

Drum Does Not Operate .... page 215

Dryer Does Not Heat .... page 217

Noisy Dryer .... page 219

How to Check Wall Outlet

- Unplug dryer.
- Readjust circuit breaker or fuse.
- Plug in appliance that is known to operate properly.
- If fuse continues to blow, check amp rating of other appliances operating on same power line.
- Total amps per wall outlet should not be more than 15 amps for most home outlets.
- If necessary, turn off appliances until appropriate total amp rate is reached.

How to Check Door Switch

- Unplug dryer.
- Disassemble dryer and expose door switch.
- Preset volt-ohmmeter to RX 1 scale.
- Attach volt-ohmmeter probes to switch contacts.
- Turn on switch.
- Volt-ohmmeter should indicate zero. If not, replace switch.

How to Check Power Cord

- Unplug dryer.
- Disassemble dryer and expose dryer end of power cord.
- Preset volt-ohmmeter to RX 1 scale.
- Attach jumper wire to dryer end of power cord. (See Illustration 1-2.)
- Attach volt-ohmmeter probes to power cord prongs.
- Volt-ohmmeter should indicate zero. If not, replace cord.

How to Check On-Off Switch

- Unplug dryer.
- Disassemble dryer and expose on-off switch.
- Preset volt-ohmmeter to RX 1 scale.
- Attach volt-ohmmeter probes to switch contacts.
- Turn on switch.
- Volt-ohmmeter should indicate zero. If not, replace cord.

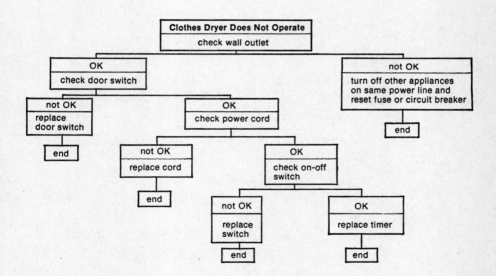

How to Check the Drum Belt

- Unplug dryer.
- Manually turn drum.
- If flapping noise is heard while turning, replace belt.
- If drum turns freely, replace belt.

How to Check Idler Unit

- Unplug dryer.
- Disassemble dryer and expose idler unit.
- Examine idler unit for loose and worn parts.
- Replace unit if necessary.

How to Check Drum for Obstruction

- Unplug dryer.
- Disassemble dryer and expose complete drum system.
- Examine all parts of the system for obstruction.
- Remove obstruction.

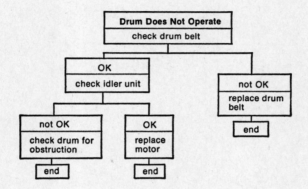

How to Check Wall Outlet

- Unplug dryer.
- Readjust circuit breaker or fuse.
- Plug in appliance that is known to operate properly.
- If fuse continues to blow, check amp rating of other appliances operating on same power line.
- Total amps per wall outlet should not be more than 15 amps for most home outlets.
- If necessary, turn off appliances until appropriate total amp rate is reached.

How to Check Lint Filter for Obstruction

- Remove lint filter.
- Examine filter for excess amount of lint.
- Clean or replace filter.

How to Check Thermostat

- Unplug dryer.
- Disassemble dryer and expose thermostat unit.
- Preset volt-ohmmeter to RX 1 scale.
- Attach volt-ohmmeter probes to thermostat contacts.
- Turn on thermostat.
- Volt-ohmmeter should indicate zero to low ohms. If not, replace thermostat.

How to Check Timer

- Unplug dryer.
- Disassemble dryer and expose timer.
- Preset volt-ohmmeter to RX 1 scale.
- Attach volt-ohmmeter probes to timer contacts.

- Set timer to dry.
- Volt-ohmmeter should indicate zero. If not, replace timer.

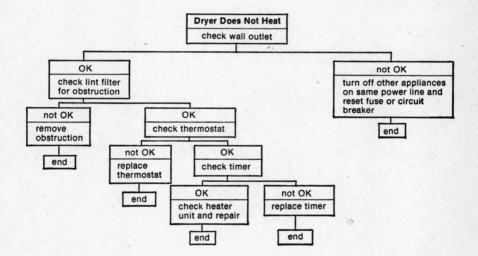

How to Check Drum for Loose Objects

- Open drum door.
- Examine surface of drum for loose objects.
- Remove objects.

How to Check Drum Belt

- Unplug dryer.
- Manually turn drum.
- If flapping noise is heard while turning, replace belt.
- If drum turns freely, replace belt.

How to Check Pulley

- Unplug dryer.
- Disassemble and expose pulley system.
- Examine every part in system.
- Replace all loose or worn parts.

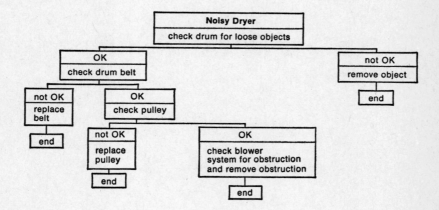

How a Dehumidifier Works

On hot, humid days the temperature seems to multiply. Moisture in the air adds to the discomfort. The more moisture or humidity, the more discomfort for the homeowner. To reduce the discomfort, two types of appliances are used: the air conditioner and the dehumidifier. Both operate in a similar manner. (See Illustration 2-2.)

Moisture in the room's air collects in a unit called the collecting coil. The coil "traps" moisture in the same manner as moisture is collected on a cold glass of beer. Air conditioners have a similar device called an evaporator coil. Water drops from the collector coil flow into a pan below the appliance floor. At this point heat from the condenser unit vaporizes the moisture and the process begins again. Air conditioners also cause vaporization; however, the vapor is forced out of the house, thereby giving additional cooling to the room.

Like any appliance, the dehumidifier will operate for years if properly maintained. Every year the unit should be cleaned. Coils in the compressor and the collector must be free of obstructions, especially dust. A vacuum cleaner will usually do the trick here. Some motors are permanently lubricated. However, examine the owner's manual to determine the type of motor that is installed in the unit. If the unit does not contain a permanently lubricated motor, lubricate every year before the season begins.

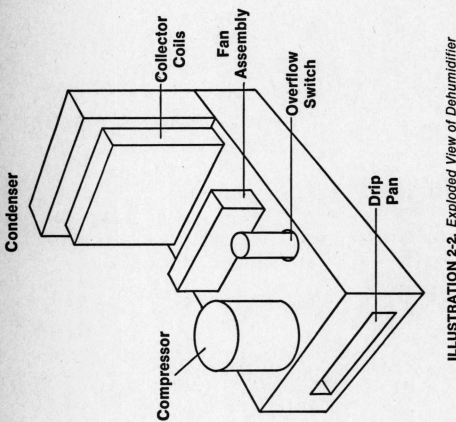

Condenser

Collector Coils

Fan Assembly

Overflow Switch

Compressor

Drip Pan

ILLUSTRATION 2-2. *Exploded View of Dehumidifier*

DIAGNOSING THE DEHUMIDIFIER

PROBLEMS

Dehumidifier Does Not Operate .... page 225

Unit Does Not Dehumidify .... page 227

Noisy Dehumidifier .... page 227

How to Check Wall Outlet

- Unplug dehumidifier.
- Readjust circuit breaker or fuse.
- Plug in appliance that is known to operate properly.
- If fuse continues to blow, check amp rating of other appliances operating on same power line.
- Total amps per wall outlet should not be more than 15 amps for most home outlets.
- If necessary, turn off appliances until appropriate total amp rate is reached.

How to Check Power Cord

- Unplug dehumidifier.
- Disassemble dehumidifier and expose dehumidifier end of power cord.
- Preset volt-ohmmeter to RX 1 scale.
- Attach jumper wire to dehumidifier end of power cord. (See Illustration 1-2.)
- Attach volt-ohmmeter probes to power cord prongs.
- Volt-ohmmeter should indicate zero. If not, replace cord.

How to Check Overflow Switch

- Unplug dehumidifier.
- Disassemble dehumidifier and expose overflow switch.
- Preset volt-ohmmeter to RX 1 scale.
- Attach volt-ohmmeter probes to overflow switch connection.
- Fill drip container with water.
- Insert overflow switch in drip container.
- Volt-ohmmeter should indicate zero. If not, replace overflow switch.

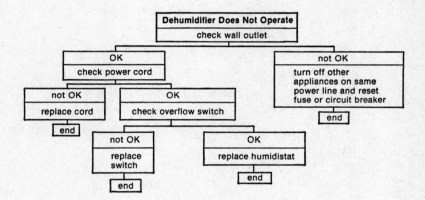

How to Check Fan Motor

- Unplug dehumidifier.
- Disassemble dehumidifier and expose motor.
- Disconnect relay.
- Preset volt-ohmmeter to RX 1 scale.
- Attach volt-ohmmeter probes to motor connection.
- Volt-ohmmeter should indicate 3 to 25 ohms. If not, replace motor.

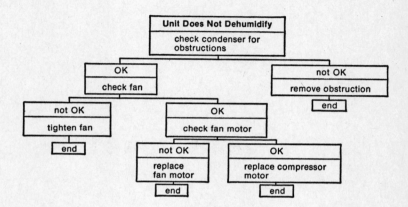

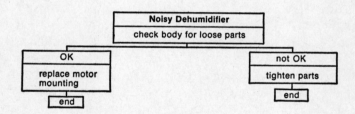

How a Dishwasher Works

Washing dishes can be a chore in some households, but others let the dishwasher handle the job. Although less conversational, a dishwasher can permit everyone to partake in activities after supper. (See Illustration 2-3.)

Although dishwashers are marketed in some variations, most operate on the same principle. Current from the power cord activates a switch/selector unit and the washer motor. When the load is ready for washing, the switch/selector is depressed. Current then flows to the intake valve solenoid. The solenoid is an electromagnet. When activated, the magnet attracts a needle-like device in the valve cylinder, allowing water to flow into the washer. Once the flow begins, the valve's second mechanism turns off the water when the desired level is reached. This second mechanism is a float switch unit. As the float rises on a shaft, it completes an electrical connection, turning off the valve.

Because the washing process involves several steps at different times, manufacturers install a time unit. This consists of a series of electrical contacts and a timer. As the timer revolves, various switch contacts are connected, turning on each mechanism individually.

Once the water level has reached the desired height and the intake valve is turned off, the motor is activated. Water from the valve enters the pump unit based on the motor shaft. Two spraying arms, one on the motor shaft and the other on the top of the washer, send water under pressure to the dishes. A detergent dispenser proportionately mixes detergent with water to assist in cleaning the dishes.

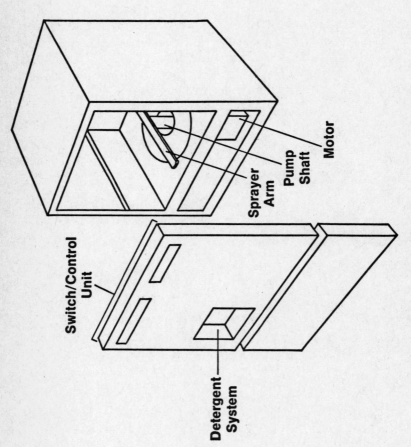

Switch/Control Unit

Sprayer Arm

Pump Shaft

Motor

Detergent System

ILLUSTRATION 2-3. *Exploded View of Dishwasher*

DIAGNOSING THE DISHWASHER

PROBLEMS

Dishwasher Does Not Operate............... page 233

Water Stays in Washer...................... page 233

Water Does Not Enter Washer .... page 235

Washer is Noisy............................. page 235

Dishwasher Does Not Wash................. page 237

How to Check Wall Outlet

- Unplug dishwasher.
- Readjust circuit breaker or fuse.
- Plug in appliance that is known to operate properly.
- If fuse continues to blow, check amp rating of other appliances operating on same power line.
- Total amps per wall outlet should not be more than 15 amps for most home outlets.
- If necessary, turn off appliances until appropriate total amp rate is reached.

How to Check Door Switch

- Unplug dishwasher.
- Disassemble unit to expose door switch.
- Preset volt-ohmmeter to RX 1 scale.
- Attach volt-ohmmeter probes to switch contacts.
- Turn on switch.
- Volt-ohmmeter should indicate zero. If not, replace switch.

How to Check Drain

- Unplug dishwasher.
- Locate drain and examine for obstruction.
- Remove obstruction.

How to Check Pump for Obstruction

- Unplug dishwasher.
- Manually turn pump shaft.
- If shaft does not move freely, examine for obstruction.
- Remove obstruction.

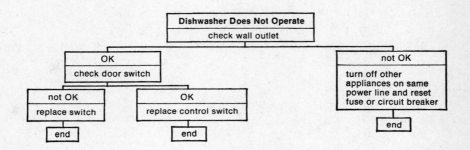

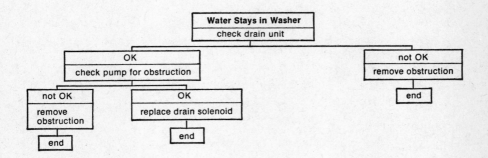

How to Check Float Switch

- Unplug dishwasher.
- Disassemble dishwasher and expose float and float switch.
- Preset volt-ohmmeter to RX 1 scale.
- Attach volt-ohmmeter probes to switch connections.
- Lower float.
- Volt-ohmmeter should indicate zero or low ohms. If not, replace switch.

How to Check Valve Screen

- Unplug dishwasher
- Disassemble to expose valve.
- Examine valve screen for obstruction.
- Remove obstruction.

How to Check Control Switch

- Unplug dishwasher.
- Disassemble dishwasher to expose switch.
- Preset volt-ohmmeter to RX 1 scale.
- Attach volt-ohmmeter probes to switch contacts.
- Turn on switch.
- Volt-ohmmeter should indicate low to zero ohms. If not, replace switch.

How to Check Water Level

- Plug in dishwasher.
- Turn on dishwasher and allow to fill.
- When water stops entering washer, examine level.
- Compare water level with water level suggested by manufacturer.

● If water level is low, turn off all faucets in house while using dishwasher.

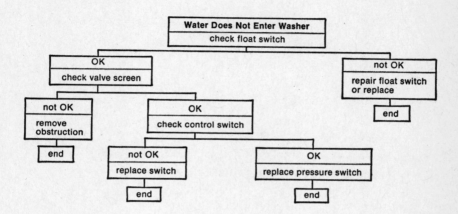

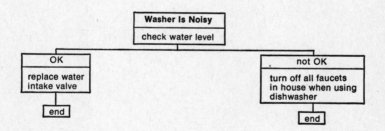

How to Check Hot Water

- Turn on hot water in sink.
- If water is not hot, check water heater and repair if necessary.
- If water is hot at sink, examine dishwasher water supply and repair.

How to Check Strainer

- Unplug dishwasher.
- Disassemble dishwasher to expose strainer.
- Examine strainer for obstruction.
- Remove obstruction.

How to Check Detergent Supply Unit

- Unplug dishwasher.
- Disassemble dishwasher and expose detergent supply system.
- Remove detergent.
- Examine detergent route for obstruction.
- Remove obstruction.

How to Check Pump

- Unplug dishwasher.
- Disassemble dishwasher.
- Manually turn pump shaft.
- If pump shaft does not turn freely, examine and remove obstruction.
- If not obstructed, replace pump.

How to Check Control Switch

- Unplug dishwasher.
- Disassemble dishwasher to expose switch.
- Preset volt-ohmmeter to RX 1 scale.
- Attach volt-ohmmeter probes to switch contacts.
- Turn on switch.
- Volt-ohmmeter should indicate low to zero ohms. If not, replace switch.

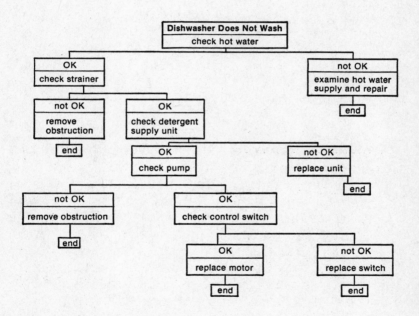

How a Room Air Conditioner Works

Air conditioners are basically the reverse of the heating system. In the heating system, air is heated by a source. Heat is then transferred through the system to a radiator or radiator-type device. Air current in the room flows through the coils in the radiator, transferring the heat to the environment. In an air conditioner, heat is collected in the evaporator and transferred to a refrigerant called freon. Under compression supplied by the compressor, the freon containing the heat is transferred to the condenser, where another heat transfer occurs. Heat leaves the freon and is blown by the condenser fan to the outside of the house. (See Illustration 2-4.)

Most air conditioners contain at least three controlling devices: the on-off switch, the thermostat, and the overload switch. While the on-off switch connects the circuit to the power cord, the thermostat, through a bimetal contact, maintains the room temperature at the desired setting.

When the temperature falls below the setting, making the room too cool, the thermostat contact cuts off the cooling system. The reverse occurs when the temperature again returns to the desired temperature. If at any time the unit becomes overloaded, the air conditioner overload switch will automatically disconnect the unit. The switch must be reset manually.

There are a few areas that should be considered in a maintenance program. Each year the evaporator and the condenser units should be checked and, if necessary, cleaned for obstructions such as dust. Also, the air conditioner filter should be cleaned regularly.

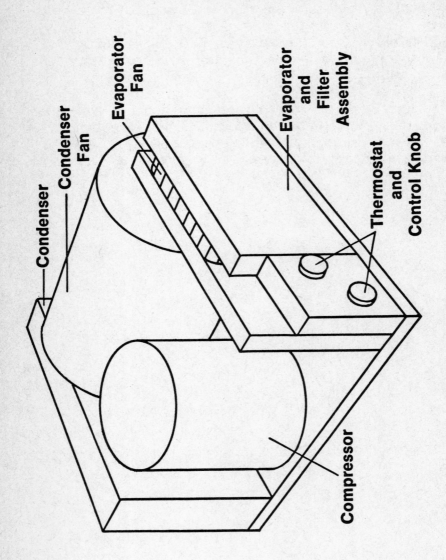

Condenser

Condenser Fan

Evaporator Fan

Evaporator and Filter Assembly

Thermostat and Control Knob

Compressor

ILLUSTRATION 2-4. *Exploded View of Room Air Conditioner*

DIAGNOSING THE AIR CONDITIONER

PROBLEMS

Air Conditioner Does Not Operate . . . . page 243

Air Conditioner Does Not Cool . . . . page 245

Noisy Air Conditioner . . . . page 245

How to Check Wall Outlet

- Unplug air conditioner.
- Readjust circuit breaker or fuse.
- Plug in appliance that is known to operate properly.
- If fuse continues to blow, check amp rating of other appliances operating on same power line.
- Total amps per wall outlet should not be more than 15 amps for most home outlets.
- If necessary, turn off appliances until appropriate total amp rate is reached.

How to Check Power Cord

- Unplug air conditioner.
- Disassemble air conditioner and expose air conditioner end of power cord.
- Preset volt-ohmmeter to RX 1 scale.
- Attach jumper wire to air conditioner end of power cord. (See Illustration 1-2.)
- Attach volt-ohmmeter probes to power cord prongs.
- Volt-ohmmeter should indicate zero. If not, replace cord.

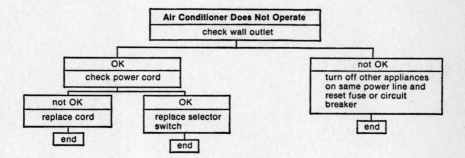

How to Check Thermostat

- Unplug air conditioner.
- Disassemble air conditioner and expose thermostat.
- Attach volt-ohmmeter probes to thermostat connections.
- Preset volt-ohmmeter to RX 1 scale.
- Turn thermostat to high.
- Volt-ohmmeter should indicate zero to low ohms. If not, replace thermostat.

How to Check Overload Switch

- Examine overload switch.
- If switch is in "off" position, turn switch on.

How to Check Condenser for Obstruction

- Unplug air conditioner.
- Examine condenser unit for dust or other obstruction.
- Remove obstruction.

How to Check Installation

- Unplug air conditioner.
- Examine mounting assembly for loose parts.
- Tighten loose parts.

How to Repair Evaporator

- Examine evaporator blades.
- If blades are not straight, unplug air conditioner and straighten blades.

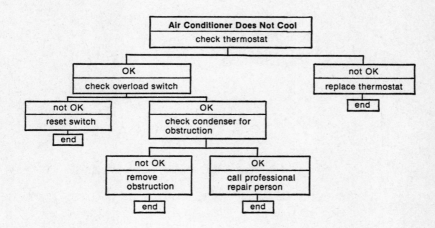

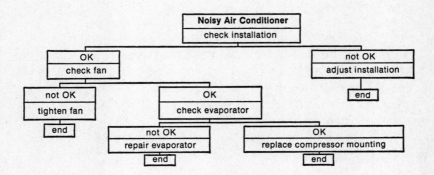

How a Humidifier Works

During the winter months when the temperature inside the house is warm, there is a natural absence of humidity or moisture in the air. The lack of humidity is seen in homes where steam heat generates the warmth. A low humidity in a house can make day-to-day chores uncomfortable, since our bodies react to the reduced moisture in the air. At such times, a humidifier can be called on to add humidity to room air. (See Illustration 2-5.)

The humidifier operates on a very basic principle. Water contained in a reservoir moistens either a drum or a belt. The drum or belt, depending upon the type of model, rotates in front of a fan. Air current powered by the fan blows through the drum or belt, "blowing" water droplets into the surrounding air. Most humidifiers only operate when there is water present in the reservoir. To control this operation, manufacturers install a float switch. The float will automatically lower with the level of water in the reservoir. When the level is below a predetermined setting, the float switch will deactivate the humidifier.

The water level of the humidifier should be checked before every operation of the unit. After the low-humidity season is over, water should be removed from the humidifier before storage. To prevent stale odors, the humidifier reservoir and the belt or drum should be washed and completely dried before retiring the unit for the season.

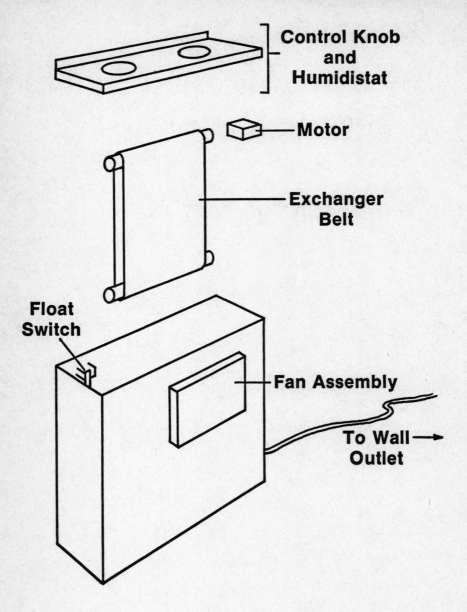

ILLUSTRATION 2-5. *Exploded View of Humidifier*

DIAGNOSING THE HUMIDIFIER

PROBLEMS

Humidifier Does Not Operate................ page 251

Noisy Humidifier............................ page 253

Humidifier Does Not Humidify.............. page 253

How to Check Wall Outlet

- Unplug humidifier.
- Readjust circuit breaker or fuse.
- Plug in appliance that is known to operate properly.
- If fuse continues to blow, check amp rating of other appliances operating on same power line.
- Total amps per wall outlet should not be more than 15 amps for most home outlets.
- If necessary, turn off appliances until appropriate total amp rate is reached

How to Check Power Cord

- Unplug humidifier.
- Disassemble humidifier.
- Preset volt-ohmmeter to RX 1 scale.
- Attach jumper wire to humidifier end of power cord. (See Illustration 1-2.)
- Attach volt-ohmmeter probes to power cord prongs.
- Volt-ohmmeter should indicate zero. If not, replace power cord.

How to Check Float Switch

- Unplug humidifier.
- Disassemble humidifier and expose float switch.
- Preset volt-ohmmeter to RX 1 scale.
- Attach volt-ohmmeter probes to switch contacts.
- Push float to top of unit.
- Volt-ohmmeter should indicate zero.

How to Check Humidistat

- Unplug humidifier.

- Disassemble humidifier and expose humidistat.
- Preset volt-ohmmeter to RX 1 scale.
- Turn humidistat to low position.
- Attach volt-ohmmeter probes to humidistat contacts.
- Volt-ohmmeter should indicate high ohms. If not, replace humidistat.

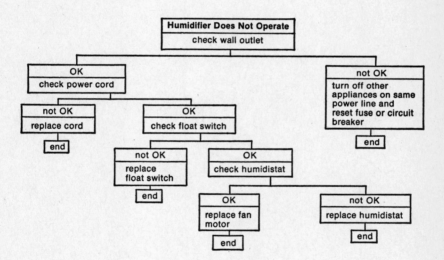

How to Check Drive System

- Unplug humidifier.
- Disassemble humidifier and expose drive system.
- Examine drive system for obstruction and clean.

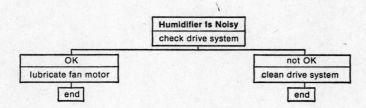

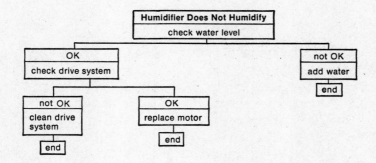

How a Refrigerator
Works

To cool off in the hot months, some people open the refrigerator door and let the "cold air" do the job. Although the refrigerator does poor duty as an air conditioner, both units do operate similarly. (See Illustration 2-6.)

A refrigerator operates in the reverse of a heater. In a heater, fluid absorbs heat from a source and carries the heat to a radiator, where there is a transfer of heat to the air. In a refrigerator, heat is absorbed from the area which is to be cooled. The refrigerant, which "carries" the heat, transfers the heat to the air outside the subject area. This transfer takes place in a unit called a condenser, similar to a radiator.

The refrigerant is under constant pressure supplied by the compressor, which is usually located at the bottom of the refrigerator. To control the temperature in the refrigerator, manufacturers install a thermostat switch. Through the use of a bimetal contact, the unit is turned on and off. The contact reaches the desired cooling temperature and breaks the connection. When the unit becomes warm, above the desired temperature, the bimetal contact connects the circuit, restoring power to the refrigerator.

During this process moisture will be developed through a natural reaction in the exchange system. Water is contained in the drainage system, which consists of a drain hose and pan. From time to time the drain pan should be cleaned and the condenser coils behind the refrigerator should be dusted.

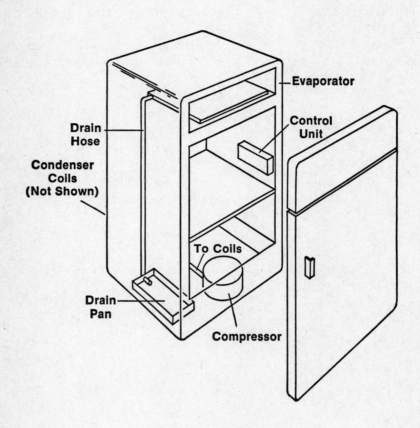

ILLUSTRATION 2-6. *Exploded View of Refrigerator*

DIAGNOSING THE REFRIGERATOR

PROBLEMS

Refrigerator Does Not Operate .... page 259

Noisy Refrigerator........................... page 261

Refrigerator Does Not Defrost............... page 261

Refrigerator Continuously Operates .... page 263

How to Check Wall Outlet

- Unplug refrigerator.
- Readjust circuit breaker or fuse.
- Plug in appliance that is known to operate properly.
- If fuse continues to blow, check amp rating of other appliances operating on same power line.
- Total amps per wall outlet should not be more than 15 amps for most home outlets.
- If necessary, turn off appliances until appropriate total amp rate is reached.

How to Check Power Cord

- Unplug refrigerator.
- Disassemble refrigerator.
- Preset volt-ohmmeter to RX 1 scale.
- Attach jumper wire to refrigerator end of power cord. (See Illustration 1-2.)
- Attach volt-ohmmeter probes to power cord prongs.
- Volt-ohmmeter should indicate zero. If not, replace power cord.

How to Check Temperature Control Unit

- Unplug refrigerator.
- Disassemble refrigerator until temperature control is exposed.
- Preset volt-ohmmeter to RX 1 scale.
- Attach volt-ohmmeter probes to temperature control connections.
- Volt-ohmmeter should indicate zero. If not, replace temperature control unit.

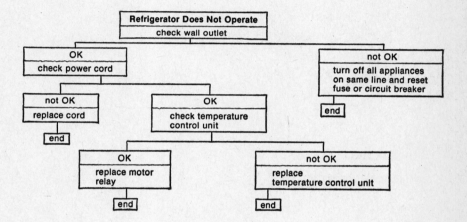

How to Check Drain Pan

- Unplug refrigerator.
- Disassemble refrigerator until drain pan is exposed.
- Examine drain pan to ensure that the pan is in correct position. If not, adjust pan.

How to Check Fan Blades for Obstruction

- Unplug refrigerator.
- Disassemble refrigerator and expose fan blades.
- Manually turn fan blades.
- If fan does not move freely, examine and remove obstruction.

How to Check Door

- Examine door for misalignment.
- Adjust door if necessary.
- Close door.
- Slip a piece of paper between door gasket and refrigerator body.
- If paper moves freely, replace door gasket.

How to Check Defroster Heater

- Unplug refrigerator.
- Disassemble refrigerator and expose defroster heater.
- Preset volt-ohmmeter to RX 1 scale
- Attach volt-ohmmeter probes to heater connections.
- Volt-ohmmeter should indicate low to zero. If not, replace defroster heater.

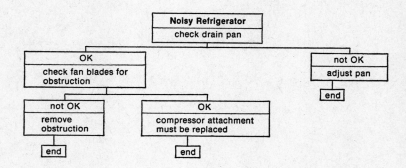

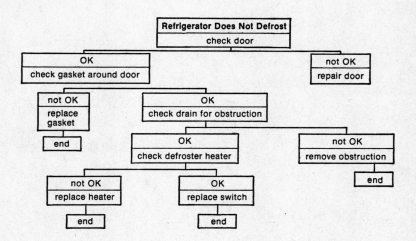

How to Check Door

- Examine door for misalignment.
- Adjust door if necessary.
- Close door.
- Slip a piece of paper between door gasket and refrigerator body.
- If paper moves freely, replace door gasket.

How to Check Condenser Unit

- Unplug refrigerator.
- Examine condenser unit for dust and dirt.
- Remove dust or dirt with vacuum cleaner.

How to Check Light Unit

- Unplug refrigerator.
- Disassemble refrigerator and expose light unit.
- Preset volt-ohmmeter to RX 1 scale.
- Attach volt-ohmmeter probes to light unit connection.
- Volt-ohmmeter should indicate zero. If not, replace light unit.

How to Check Fan Blades for Obstruction

- Unplug refrigerator.
- Disassemble refrigerator and expose fan blades.
- Manually turn fan blades.
- If fan does not move freely, examine and remove obstruction.

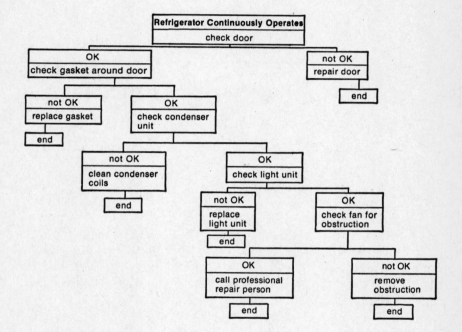

How a Sewing Machine Works

Handstitching clothes is acceptable for relatively small jobs. However, large detailed sewing requires speed and the capabilities of a machine. Sewing machines provide the versatility for professional sewing work at home.

The concepts of sewing by hand and by machine are basically the same. Thread is pulled in and out of the clothes in series. Usually, knots are tied at both ends of the thread to ensure that the cloth remains in position. The difference between manual sewing and machine sewing is how the laborious task of moving the thread through the clothes is accomplished. (See Illustration 2-7.)

In a sewing machine, current from the power cord causes the motor to rotate. Through a pulley action the drive shaft is turned. Linkage in the needle-drive compartment transfers rotational motion to vertical motion in the needle. Depending upon the model, the needle drive unit may also move the needle in various directions to allow for attractive stitching. Thread used for stitching is contained in the bobbin unit, below the sewing floor and the spool feed. The thread is either manually or automatically inserted into the needle. Since each type of thread will be able to remain intact under certain tension, usually the pull of the needle, manufacturers install a tension gauge. By setting the tension gauge to the appropriate selection determined by the type of thread used, thread should not break during sewing.

Every year moving parts of the sewing machine should be cleaned and lubricated according to manufacturer's instructions.

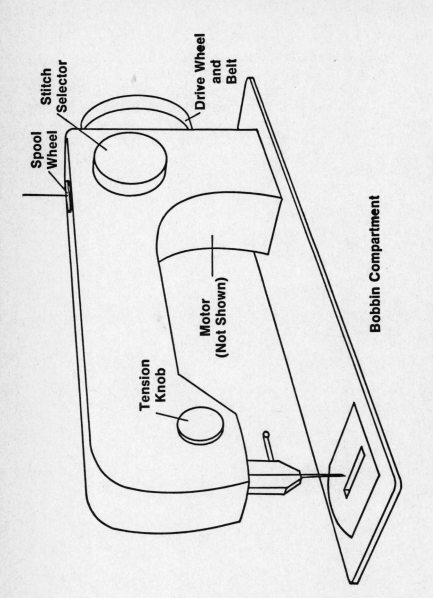

ILLUSTRATION 2-7. *Exploded View of Sewing Machine*

DIAGNOSING THE SEWING MACHINE

PROBLEMS

Sewing Machine Does Not Operate .... page 269

Needle Does Not Turn .... page 269

Thread Breaks .... page 271

Needle Breaks .... page 271

How to Check Wall Outlet

- Unplug sewing machine.
- Readjust circuit breaker or fuse.
- Plug in appliance that is known to operate properly.
- If fuse continues to blow, check amp rating of other appliances operating on same power line.
- Total amps per wall outlet should not be more than 15 amps for most home outlets.
- If necessary, turn off appliances until appropriate total amp rate is reached.

How to Check Power Cord

- Unplug sewing machine.
- Disassemble sewing machine and expose sewing machine end of power cord.
- Attach jumper wire to sewing machine side of power cord. (See Illustration 1-2.)
- Attach volt-ohmmeter probes to power cord prongs.
- Volt-ohmmeter should indicate zero. If not, replace power cord.

How to Check Belt

- Examine belt.
- If belt is too loose, tighten belt.
- If belt is too tight, loosen belt.
- Replace belt if worn.

How to Check Bobbin Switch Position

- Examine bobbin switch.
- When stitching with sewing machine, bobbin switch should be turned off.
- When threading bobbin, bobbin switch should be activated.

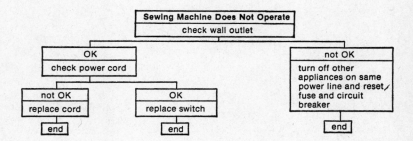

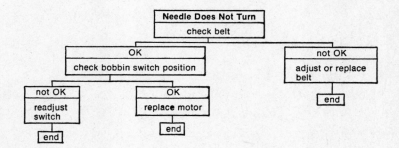

How to Check Threading Procedures

- Since each model is different, check with owner's manual received when machine was purchased.
- If owner's manual is not available, contact manufacturer's customer assistance department.

How to Check Needle

- Unplug sewing machine.
- Examine the position of the needle in the needle hold-down unit.
- If needle is not snug, adjust needle.
- Examine needle size. Check with manufacturer's instructions for proper needle size for specific thread gauge.
- Examine the condition of needle. Needle must be straight. If not, replace needle.

How to Check Tension Gauge Setting

- If thread breaks, relieve the tension by decreasing setting on tension gauge.

How to Check Needle

- Unplug sewing machine.
- Examine the position of needle in the needle hold-down unit.
- If needle is not snug, adjust needle.
- Examine needle size. Check with manufacturer's instructions for proper needle size for specific thread gauge.
- Examine the condition of needle. Needle must be straight. If not, replace needle.

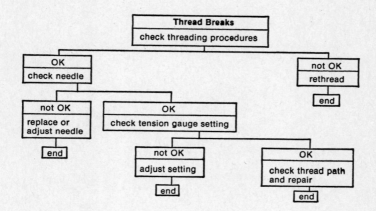

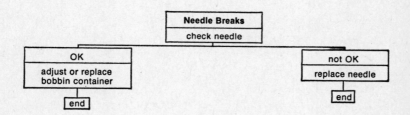

How a Stove Works

There are basically two types of stoves on the market. They are the gas range and the electric range. As the names indicate, the difference in the units is the method by which heat is transferred from a supply to the food. (See Illustration 2-8.)

In the gas stove, natural gas is fed into the system from a public source, usually the utility company, Gas alone will not burn. For a flame to exist, gas must be properly mixed with the oxygen in air. The gas stove is the mechanical unit that mixes and controls the gas/air fuel. Behind the stove is a gas pipe fitted with a valve. Usually there is another gas valve in the system where the service enters the building. In emergencies or when the stove must be moved, either valve can be used to disconnect the flow of gas.

Gas flows through an internal pipe system in the stove. A fine flame constantly burns. This is called a pilot light. The purpose of a pilot light is to enable quick lighting of the burners without having to light a match every time the stove is to be used. Once the gas/air mixture is set at the shutter, the heating dial feeds the flame greater amounts of the fuel mixture as required.

In an electric stove, there are no outside connections except for a power cord. Current from the wall outlet enters a thermostat which controls the amount of heat that is to be generated. Heat is provided by resistances to current in the heating element. To move the electric stove, the user will only have to turn the stove switch off and remove the plug.

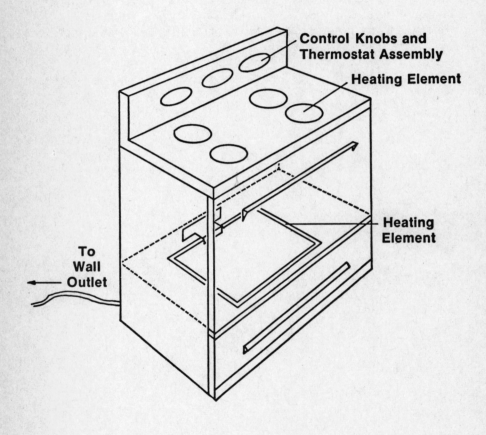

ILLUSTRATION 2-8. *Exploded View of Electric Stove*

DIAGNOSING THE STOVE

PROBLEMS

Electric Stove Does Not Operate .... page 277

Electric Stove Does Not Heat .... page 277

Gas Stove Does Not Operate................ page 279

How to Check Wall Outlet

- Unplug stove.
- Readjust circuit breaker or fuse.
- Plug in appliance that is known to operate properly. (You may need a special plug if stove uses 240v.)
- If fuse continues to blow, check amp rating of other appliances operating on same power line.
- Total amps per wall outlet should not be more than 15 to 30 amps for most home outlets.
- If necessary, turn off appliances until appropriate total amp rate is reached.

How to Check Heating Element

- Unplug range.
- Disassemble range and expose heating element.
- Preset volt-ohmmeter to RX 1 scale.
- Attach volt-ohmmeter probes to each end of heating element.
- Volt-ohmmeter should indicate zero or low ohms. If not, replace element.

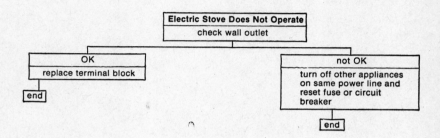

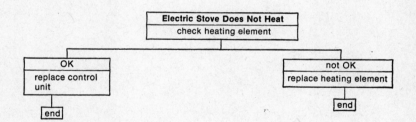

How to Check Gas Supply

- Examine gas pipe valve connection behind stove and in basement.
- If valve is off, turn valve on.

How to Check Burner Pipe

- Turn stove off.
- Carefully examine burner holes for obstruction.
- Remove obstruction.

How to Adjust Gas/Air Mixture

- Disassemble stove and expose air shutter opening.
- If flame is yellow on burner, open air shutter more.
- If flame is too high, close air shutter a little.

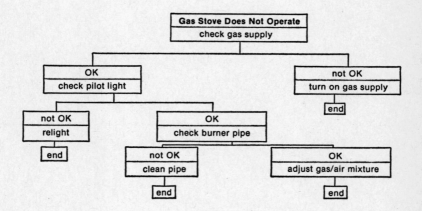

How a Washing Machine Works

The washboard is a thing of the past, of value only to collectors. However, the same principle of getting clothes clean still holds true today. Dirt collects in the fine fibers of material. Although a microscope would be required to actually see a particle of dirt, when the fibers are nearly saturated with it, the situation becomes noticeable and clothes are quickly headed for the wash.

The electric washing machine handles the awesome chore of removing dirt. (See Illustration 2-9.) Clothes fill the washer drum along with water from the house water supply. Usually both hot and cold water fill the drum, after which detergent is added. (Some manufacturers provide a self-dispensing unit in the washer which enables the proper amount of detergent to be added automatically.) The water is then agitated as the agitator forces the detergent and water through the fibers, releasing the dirt. Once the wash cycle is completed, a pump drains the water from the drum, fresh water enters, and the rinse cycle begins.

Washing machines are controlled by two devices: the timer, which determines which cycle should be activated at the proper time, and the temperature switch, which determines the amount of hot and cold water mixture to flow into the drum.

To prevent unnecessary breakdowns, there are several checks that should be made every year. Hoses and belts can easily break and loosen. Examine all belts and hoses and also lubricate moving parts.

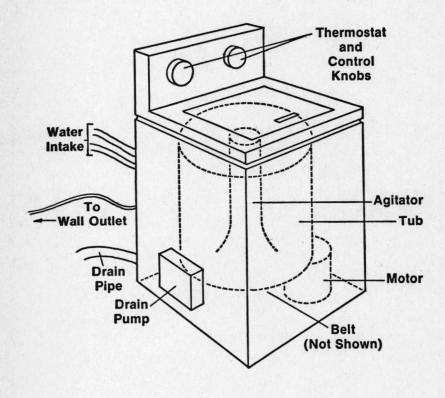

ILLUSTRATION 2-9. *Exploded View of Washing Machine*

DIAGNOSING THE WASHING MACHINE

PROBLEMS

Water Does Not Enter Unit.................... page 285

Washing Machine Does Not Operate......... page 287

Washing Machine Does Not Spin............ page 287

Washing Machine Is Noisy................... page 289

How to Check Wall Outlet

- Unplug washing machine.
- Readjust circuit breaker or fuse.
- Plug in appliance that is known to operate properly.
- If fuse continues to blow, check amp rating of other appliances operating on same power line.
- Total amps per wall outlet should not be more than 15 amps for most home outlets.
- If necessary, turn off appliances until appropriate total amp rate is reached.

How to Check Water Hose

- If necessary, disassemble washing machine and expose water hose system.
- Examine hose for wear, leaks, and obstructions.
- Repair or replace hose.

How to Check Valve Screen

- Unplug washing machine.
- Disassemble washing machine and expose valve screen.
- Examine screen and remove any obstructions or replace screen.

How to Check Power Cord

- Unplug washing machine.
- Disassemble washing machine and expose washing machine end of power cord.
- Preset volt-ohmmeter to RX 1 scale.
- Attach jumper wire to washing machine end of power cord. (See Illustration 1-2.)

- Attach volt-ohmmeter probes to power cord prongs.
- Volt-ohmmeter should indicate zero. If not, replace power cord.

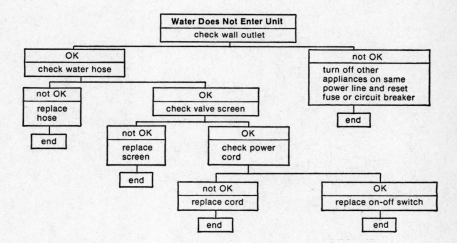

How to Check Door Switch

- Unplug washing machine.
- Disassemble washing machine and expose door switch.
- Preset volt-ohmmeter to RX 1 scale.
- Attach volt-ohmmeter probes to switch contacts.
- Turn on switch.
- Volt-ohmmeter should indicate zero. If not, replace switch.

How to Check if Drum Is Overloaded

- Open washer door.
- Examine position of clothes.
- If clothes are all to one side of drum, redistribute clothes evenly.
- If overload switch turned off washing machine, reset switch.

How to Check Drive Belt

- Unplug washing machine.
- Disassemble washing machine and expose drive belt.
- Examine drive belt. If worn, replace belt.
- Depress drive belt approximately ¾".
- If belt moved more than ¾", tighten belt.
- If belt moved less than ¾", loosen belt.

How to Check Spin Solenoid

- Unplug washing machine.
- Disassemble washing machine and expose solenoid.
- Preset volt-ohmmeter to RX 1 scale.

- Attach volt-ohmmeter probes to solenoid connections.
- Volt-ohmmeter should indicate 275 to 900 ohms. If not, replace solenoid.

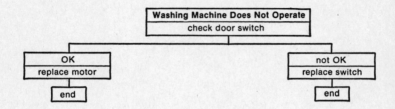

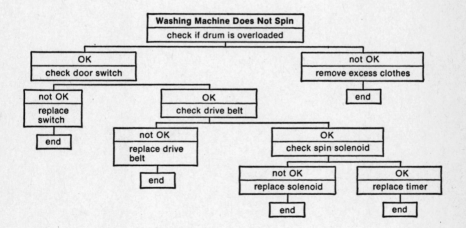

How to Check if Drum Is Overloaded

- Open washer door.
- Examine position of clothes.
- If clothes are all to one side of drum, redistribute clothes evenly.
- If overload switch turned off washing machine, reset switch.

How to Check Leg Adjustment

- Turn washing machine off.
- Manually tilt washing machine.
- Examine each leg and adjust leg in direction of tilt.

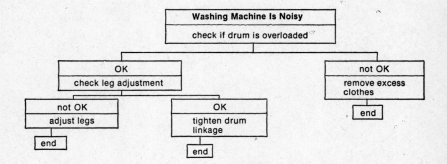

How a Waste Disposer Works

The cost of hiring a plumber to clean out the drain pipe in the kitchen can be expensive. Even a very careful wife or husband can't prevent scraps from finding their way down the drain and clogging the water path. To facilitate removal of scrap deposits, many homeowners install a waste disposer. (See Illustration 2-10.)

A waste disposer is mounted under the sink, in line with the drain pipes. As water and scraps flow down the drain, the unit, activated by either a wall switch or a stopper, will start the grinding wheel, shredding food scraps into smaller pieces that can be easily disposed through the house drainage system.

Waste disposers are designed to shred food scraps, but not thicker objects. From time to time the disposer will jam. Usually a few good jars to the flywheel with a broom handle will do the trick. However, there are several common causes of disposer jamming, most of which can be prevented. Never allow glass pieces or metal objects to fall into the disposer, especially while the unit is in operation. To do so could cause serious damage to the unit.

When a waste disposer is installed in the sink drainage system, there is no need to use drain cleaners. The disposer will keep the drains relatively clean. Most important is to use caution when working on the unit, even if you are just removing an obstruction. Always turn off the disposer and never place your hand in the unit to remove an obstruction.

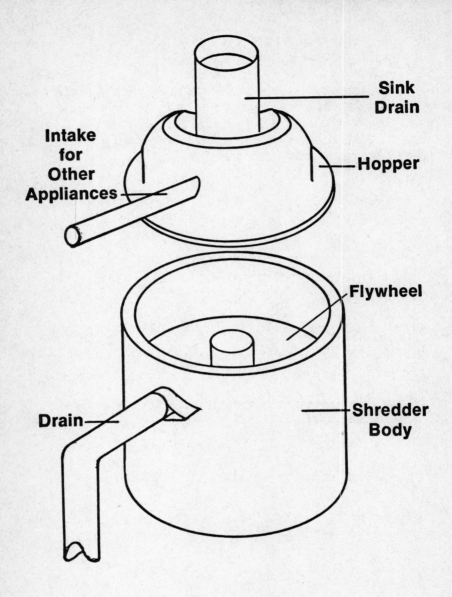

ILLUSTRATION 2-10. *Exploded View of Waste Disposer*

DIAGNOSING THE WASTE DISPOSER

PROBLEMS

Waste Disposer Does Not Operate .... page 295

Waste Disposer Too Slow .... page 295

Unit Leaks .... page 295

How to Check Wall Outlet

- Unplug waste disposer.
- Readjust circuit breaker or fuse.
- Plug in appliance that is known to operate properly.
- If fuse continues to blow, check amp rating of other appliances operating on same power line.
- Total amps per wall outlet should not be more than 15 amps for most home outlets.
- If necessary, turn off appliances until appropriate total amp rate is reached.

How to Check Waste Overload

- Locate waste overload switch and depress it.

How to Check Water Flow

- Activate disposer.
- Run water.
- Disposer should speed up.

How to Check Pipe Connection

- Activate disposer.
- Examine pipe connections.
- If necessary, tighten connection and apply putty.

How to Check Sink Gasket

- Locate sink gasket.
- Tighten gasket hold-down.

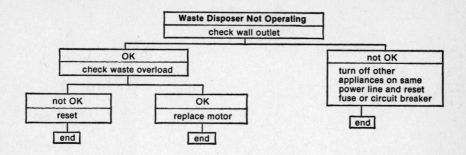

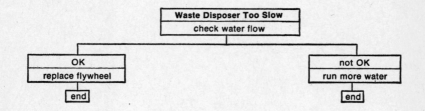

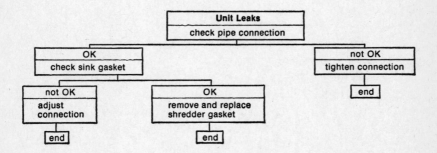

Appendix A

Tips on Home Electricity

Things to Know About Electricity

Power supplied to your home is generated at a local or regional power plant, where current is then fed along various power lines to the entrance panel in your home. The entrance panel is more commonly called the fuse panel or circuit breaker panel located in the basement.

Voltage is simply a measurement of electricity. Most modern homes have service called 120/240 volts which will handle the increasing load demand for electric power by the homeowner. Although most service from the power company is stated as 120/240, the actual voltage entering the panel will vary depending upon your location. For example, a surburban home may have 118 volts while someone in the city might have a higher rating of 208 volts.

Appliances are manufactured with a volt rating, a range in which the appliance will perform properly. In most cases the range is around 7%. As long as voltage supplied to the appliance is within 7% of 120/240, the appliance will not be damaged. However, variances beyond 7% could cause poor performance and harm the appliance. Utility companies realize the critical range, and will allow local blackouts to occur during high demand periods rather than reduce voltage on the line.

Voltage will not be the same at every wall outlet because the greater the distance from the entrance panel, the lower the voltage. Similar to the variance allowed to the utility companies, there is also a tolerance built into a home system. Using a volt-ohmmeter or an appropriate measuring device, voltage readings can be taken at the entrance panel and at a distant wall outlet. If the voltage at the outlet differs by 4 volts, inadequate wiring exists that could cause serious damage to the house and appliances. An electrician should be contacted to make the proper adjustments. A power source of 120 volts is generally used for small appliances, while 240 volts are required for larger appliances such as air conditioners and clothes dryers. All homes should have a 120/240-volt system.

About Amps

Another form of electrical measurement is called amps, or amperes. Besides the utility company supplying a specific voltage to the entrance panel, they also bring in a certain amp rating. Years ago the average house would have either 60- or 100-amp service. The 60-amp service enables the homeowner to use portable appliances, a hot water heater, and lighting, but major appliances could not be added without increasing the amp service. The 100-amp service, which is the minimum now required under the National Electric Code, which most states adopted as law, enables the homeowner to use major appliances plus lighting and up to 10,000 watts of other appliances. Today, more and more homeowners are going beyond the minimum requirements and have increased their amp service to 150 or 200 amps. The 150-amp service is required for homes that have an electric range, a high-speed dryer, and central air conditioning among the normal appliances. In 200-amp service, the capacity does not change, but adds additional amps to facilitate electric heating.

Amp service is brought into the house at the service panel. It is at this point where the service is distributed to various areas in the house. The entrance panel will have one line dropped in from the utility pole or underground entrance and then up to 22 lines of distribution. Each line contains 120 volts and either 15 or 20 amps. When 240 volts are required, two lines are used. Each line corresponds to either a fuse or a circuit breaker. The rating of the fuse or circuit breaker is the same rate as the amps drawn by that line. For example, a line with a 15-amp rating will have either a 15-amp fuse or circuit breaker. When more than 15 amps are drawn from the line, the circuit will be interrupted by the fuse or circuit breaker. By turning off power to the line, heating of the wire is prevented, reducing the possibility of a fire.

Each appliance on an in-house line will draw a certain amount of amps. (See Illustration A-1.) As long as all operating appliances on the same line do not exceed the amp rating of the line (15 or 20 amps), the line will not be overloaded and the fuse will not blow. To determine the amp draw of an appliance, another measurement of electricity and some basic math must be used. Most appliances are not rated according to amps, but are rated in terms of wattage. In general, watts equal the amps multiplied by the volts. Therefore, to determine the amount of amps an appliance will use, watts, which are rated on the appliance, are divided by volts, either 120 or 240. This will result in the amp rating for the appliance.

$$\text{amps} = \frac{\text{watts}}{\text{volts}}$$

Common watt ratings of appliances are listed as follows:

Appliance	Watts
Automatic Dryer (high-speed)	8700
Automatic Dryer (regular)	4500
Automatic Washer	700
Built-In Room Heater	1600
Central Air Conditioner	5000
Dishwasher	1800
Dishwasher-Waste Disposer	1500
Fuel-fired Heating Mechanism	800
Garbage Disposer	900
Home Freezer	350
Water Heater	2500
Water Pump	300-700

Courtesy Sears, Roebuck and Co.

Each unit may differ from ratings indicated here, but if the above ratings are used, the homeowner will be able to feel assured that the proper amp rating is identified.

How to Prevent Blown Fuses or Circuit Breakers

The most common method of preventing a blown circuit is to keep the amp load below the rating of the line. However, to prevent the need for additional amp requirements on a single power line, wall outlets should be properly placed throughout the house. For example, at least two 20-amp wall outlets should be available for the kitchen, dining room, and laundry room—areas where heavy appliance use exists. An additional 20-amp line is suggested every 500 square feet and a 15-amp line every 375 feet.

A line does not necessarily mean a wall outlet. There can be several wall outlets on one line from the entrance panel. In most cases, too many wall outlets on a single line is the cause for blown fuses. For example, a toaster may be plugged into an outlet across the room from someone using a hair dryer. Although both are plugged into two different wall outlets, a fuse blows. Both wall outlets are connected on the same line from the entrance panel. When wall outlets are connected in a series on one line, all the wall outlets together can only draw the total rate for the line, either 15 or 20 amps.

For convenience, outlets should be located every 12 feet along a wall, This will enable flexibility in rearranging furniture without the need for extension cords. The suggested distances of wall outlets differ in the kitchen, where many small appliances are frequently used. The outlets should be set about every four feet along the wall or counter. (See Illustration A-2.)

How to Select the Proper Extension Cords

When appliances are to be used in areas where wall outlets are not readily available, extension cords are used to solve the power connection problem. There are several different types of extension cords, each having a specific purpose. In general, the larger the appliance, the more of a load is drawn and, therefore, the need for larger extension cord wire exists. The reverse is also true: the smaller the appliance, the less need for large-wire extension cord.

In electrical wiring, wires are identified by sizes. To the surprise of many, the *smaller* the wire size number, the *larger* the wire. Besides the size number, wires are also rated according to load in the form of normal load and capacity load. The closer the wire reaches capacity load, the more danger exists. When the wire is near capacity, an increasing amount of heat is generated which could cause a fire.

For lamps or small appliances, extension cords should be made from No. 16 or 18 wire. For larger appliances, motors, lawn mowers, and shop tools, No. 14, 12, or 16 wire can be used. The following table can be used to determine loads for each type of wire.

wire size	normal load	capacity load
No.12	16.6 amps (1900W)	20 amps (2400 W)
No.14	12.5 amps (1500 W)	15 amps (1800 W)
No.16	8.3 amps (1000 W)	10 amps (1200 W)
No.18	5.0 amps (600 W)	7 amps (840 W)

Courtesy Sears, Roebuck and Co.

Extension cords come in various lengths, which is more important than some people might realize. The longer the cord, the more distance the appliance can be from the wall outlet; however, the greater distance increases the chance of a voltage drop. As pointed out earlier, there is a certain voltage range within which appliances will operate without causing damage to the motor. If the voltage drops below the tolerance, the appliance may not operate properly and may even malfunction. To make sure the length of the extension cord will not drop the voltage below the tolerance range, check the following table.

Wire Size Number of Extension Cord

	load to 7 amps	from 7 to 10 amps	10 to 15 amps
to 25 ft.	No. 18	No. 16	No. 14
to 50 ft.	No. 16	No. 14	No. 12
to 100 ft.	No. 14	No. 12	No. 10

Courtesy Sears, Roebuck and Co.

3 important MUSTS

1 You must install electric service with capacity to meet present and future needs

Never forget the importance of providing plently of EXTRA capacity when you plan your wiring. The size of the service entrance switch, the size of the connecting wires, determine the total amount of electricity you can use at any one time. With extra capacity, you can keep on adding new electrical servants as you need them, without fear of overloading wires or blowing fuses. A properly planned "Service Entrance" (as shown at left) including switch and connecting wires will relieve you of the annoyance and loss of power and current caused by overheated wires. Proper capacity assures you of getting top performance from your electrical tools at all times.

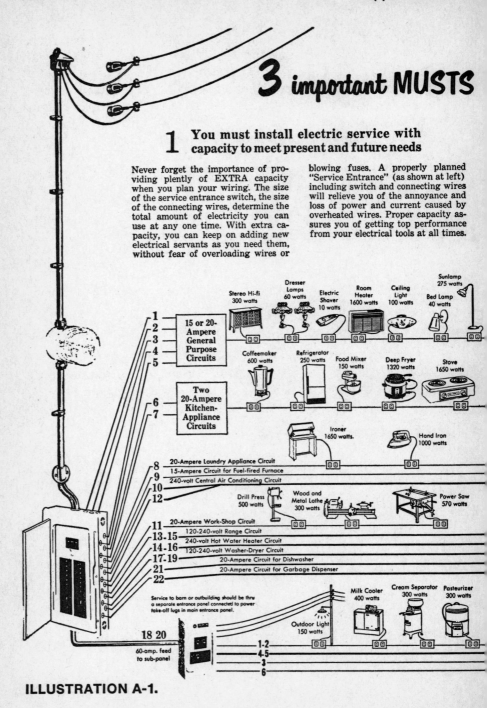

ILLUSTRATION A-1.

in planning up-to-date wiring

2 You must plan enough circuits to deliver full power always

Divide lights and outlets into various branch circuits as shown.

CODE REQUIREMENTS: all receptacles must be grounded type for new work or replacement on grounded systems. At least TWO 20-amp appliance grounded type circuits for kitchen, dining room and one for the laundry, independent of lighting fixtures.

A separate 20-amp general purpose circuit is recommended for every 500 square feet or a 15-amp circuit every 375 feet of floor space.

3 You must provide enough outlets on each circuit for convenience

A convenience outlet located every 12 feet of running wall space is required to provide complete flexibility in furniture placement, prevents unsightly long extension cords, assures better lighting.

IN KITCHENS, an outlet every 4 feet of counter space provides quick plug-in of appliances without moving them around, lets you make the most of your work space.

Be sure to plan a few outdoor outlets for holiday lighting, appliances or summer fun.

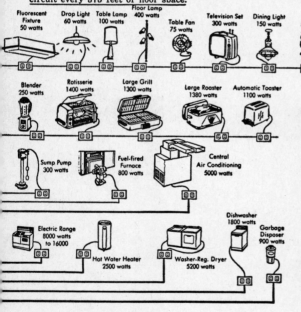

Figure total wattage for each circuit

NOTICE: Good planning insures that all outlets on a floor are not on one circuit. This prevents one blown fuse from throwing a whole floor into darkness. Note 4 circuits on 2nd floor. Note also that dining room, kitchen and laundry are on separate circuits. Put most circuits where load is heaviest.

CAUTION!

Maximum carrying capacity of a 20-ampere general-purpose or appliance circuit with. Number-12 wire is 2400 watts. Check wattages shown here. No combination of appliances exceeding that wattage should be used on any one circuit at any one time.

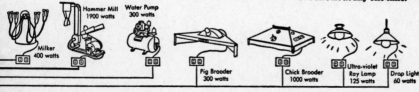

Courtesy Sears, Roebuck and Co.

Facts to help you decide which size Electric Service you should install

150 and 200 Ampere Service

Number 1/0 or number 3/0 (type RHW insulation), 3-wire Electric Service with 150 or 200-ampere service panel respectively, is preferred for modern, up-to-date wiring where full "housepower" is desired. In homes equipped with an electric range, water heater, high speed dryer or central air conditioning together with lighting and the usual small appliances, you will need a 150-ampere service as a minimum. With the addition of electric heating, a 200-ampere service is necessary.

Most farms and ranches are also finding 150 and 200-ampere service necessary using yard pole distribution.

Appliance	Watts
Fuel-fired Heating Mechanism	800
Dishwasher-Waste Disposer	1500
Central Air-conditioner	5000
Automatic Washer	700
Automatic Dryer (regular)	4500
Automatic Dryer (high-speed)	8700
Water Heater	2500
Water Pump	300 to 700
Home Freezer	350
Built-in Room Heater	1600
Garbage Disposer	900
Dishwasher	1800

A 150-ampere service provides sufficient electric capacity for lighting and portable appliances including ironer, roaster, rotisserie and refrigerator, 12000 watt range, and 8700-watt clothes dryer and also for 5000 watts (3 to 5 tons) of central or room air conditioning plus any of the appliances listed in table at left, up to 5500 watts.

A 200-ampere service provides the same capacity as the 150-ampere service but will also handle electric house heating equipment.

Modern farms and ranches, especially those with dairy and poultry operations, are best with a 200-amp. service.

100 Ampere Service

Number 2 or number 3 (type RHW insulation), 3-wire electric service with 100-ampere service panel is minimum according to the National Electric Code for homes up to 3000 square feet in floor area. In most areas, the minimum Electric Service for new homes is 100-ampere for lights, roaster, ironer, refrigerator and 8000-W. range plus appliances in table above up to 10000-W. total.

60 Ampere Service

Number 6, 3-wire Electric Service has been the standard for years but in most cases it is now too small. This service provides capacity for lighting and portable appliances including range, dryer-regular, or hot water heater but no additional major appliances can be added at any time.

30 Ampere Service

This service consists of Number 8, 2-wire Electric Service (for 120-volts only) with a 30-ampere service panel. This service provides only limited capacity for lighting and a few of the smaller appliances and should never be used except for temporary service or one room buildings. You would have to enlarge the service capacity before using any major electrical appliances.

When buying a home be sure to check the entire wiring system before you buy

When buying a new home

Be certain you check the size of the Electric Service wires and Electric Service Panel before you buy. If you are planning to build, be sure the proper size electrical service, branch circuits and outlets are specified. The additional cost of up-to-date wiring over minimum wiring is only 1% to 2% of the original cost of the home.

When buying an old home

Check the capacity of the Electric Service, panel circuits and outlets just as you check roofing, paint and general condition. A home with 3-wire service has more value than one with 2-wire service.

If you require any modification in electric wiring when moving into another home, Sears will be happy to advise you.

In existing homes

Remember that few homes 15 years or older, have been rewired for up-to-date convenience and safety. 90% of all homes need some rewiring to provide for today's needs. Check the size of your electric service, panel, circuits and outlets . . . then expand and modernize your wiring system to meet present and future needs.

These floor sketches show a typical, average-size six room home with a large basement, and containing the usual number of modern electric servants. The wiring diagrams show why at least 24 circuits are now recommended by electrical experts. It takes this many to provide adequately for proper lighting and all needed appliances, including an electric range, dishwasher, garbage disposer, water heater, power tools and central air conditioner.

ILLUSTRATION A-2.

Work Shop Circuit

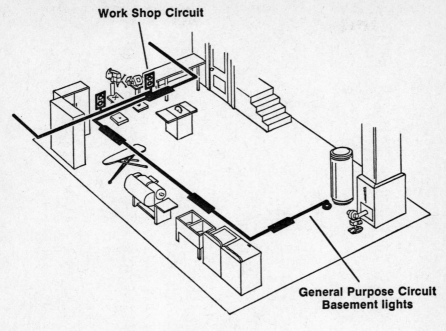

**General Purpose Circuit
Basement lights**

**Continuation of Circuit
All dining room and some
kitchen receptacles**

**General Purpose Circuit
All living room outlets
and kitchen lights**

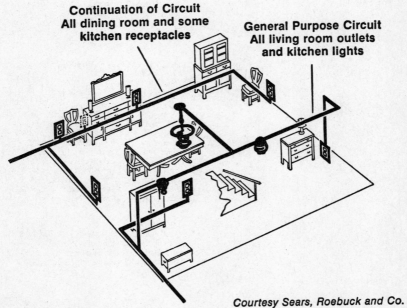

Courtesy Sears, Roebuck and Co.

ILLUSTRATION A-2. *(Continued)*

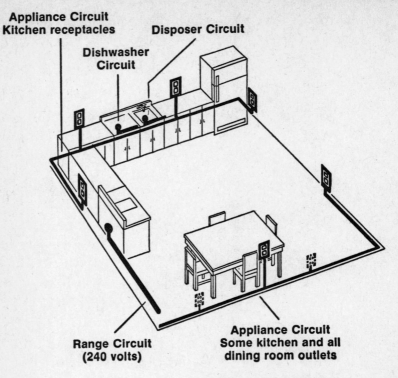

**Appliance Circuit
Kitchen receptacles**

Disposer Circuit

**Dishwasher
Circuit**

**Range Circuit
(240 volts)**

**Appliance Circuit
Some kitchen and all
dining room outlets**

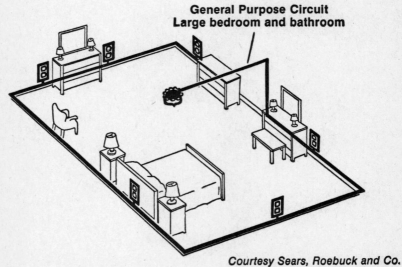

**General Purpose Circuit
Large bedroom and bathroom**

Courtesy Sears, Roebuck and Co.

ILLUSTRATION A-2. *(Continued)*

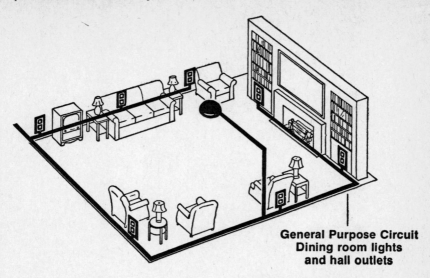

**General Purpose Circuit
Dining room lights
and hall outlets**

Courtesy Sears, Roebuck and Co.

ILLUSTRATION A-2. *(Continued)*

Appendix B

Tools of the Trade

How to Select Tools for Appliance Repair

Appliance repair, like other trades, requires tools, some that are special and others that form part of a basic tool set. Tools do not make an appliance repair person, but a person is not an appliance repair person without the proper tools. When "do-it-yourselfers" embark on a new repair, many frustrations can be alleviated through use of the right tool to do the job.

General types of tools required to repair appliances include the following:

- screwdriver (both standard and Phillips)
- vise-grip pliers
- wrenches (adjustable, open end, and box)

- channel pliers
- slip-joint pliers
- needle-nose pliers
- nut-driver set
- flashlight
- Allen wrenches
- pocket knife

Most tools used to loosen and tighten fasteners on the appliance are common to the do-it-yourselfer.

Following are some of the special tools used for appliance repair.

- volt-ohmmeter
- continuity tester
- light tester
- multipurpose tool
- soldering iron
- spring-clamp pliers
- jumper wire

The volt-ohmmeter will be discussed in detail later in this section. The *continuity tester* performs a function similar to the volt-ohmmeter. One of the major concerns in appliance repair is to find the problem in the circuit. If a circuit is completed, power will flow and usually the appliance will operate. When there is a breakdown in the circuit, it is up to the repair person to locate the trouble. There are two basic methods of determining where the problem exists in the appliance: through the use of jumper wires, which is very dangerous, and through the use of a volt-ohmmeter or continuity tester.

If the jumper wire is to be used, one end of the wire is attached to the appliance end of the power cord, with the power cord plugged into the wall outlet, and the other end of the wire is used as a probe along the circuit. Obviously, exposure to such an open circuit would be deadly. Therefore, the most common method used is the continuity tester. Instead of using high-voltage house current, the continuity tester uses low voltage in the form of a battery. Leads from the continuity tester are attached to various connections in the circuit. If the circuit is okay, the continuity light will glow. If the tester light does not operate, the circuit is broken and the problem with the appliance has been identified.

The *light tester* is used in a similar manner, only it is used primarily to check wall outlets. A light tester rated for 120 to 240 volts can be inserted into the wall outlet. If the light glows, current is flowing from the outlet. If not, the outlet is not operating.

Similar to a pair of pliers in appearance, the *multipurpose tool* is the best friend an appliance repair person can have. This tool can accurately strip insulation from almost any size wire, cut wire, crimp connections, and measure the size of the wire.

The *soldering iron* is used to make professional wire connections. Many times the repair person will have to remove and replace components of an appliance. When reinstalling the new unit, all splicing, unless otherwise indicated by manufacturer's instructions, should be soldered. When selecting a soldering iron, the most important factor to consider is the range of the unit. For appliance repair, a 25- to 50-watt soldering iron will do the job.

Countless hours have been spent by do-it-yourselfers trying to remove spring clamps, usually from hose connections. The favorite tool selected for the job is a pair of needle-nose pliers. Although this may work, the proper tool to use is a set of *spring-clamp pliers*. Because of the specially designed tips, the spring-clamp pliers can grab the spring clamp with ease.

The last tool mentioned is the *jumper wire*. This is probably the least expensive and yet one of the more important and frequently used tools in the appliance repair person's kit. Jumper wire can be made from No. 18 wire and two clamps. It is primarily used to check power cords.

The *volt-ohmmeter,* sometimes called a multimeter, is a must for anyone repairing appliances. It is used to test internal circuits as well as components in the appliance. A good volt-ohmmeter should be able to indicate both low and high ohms—the measurement of resistance. The volt-ohmmeter selector dial should contain positions for the RX 1 and RX 100 scales—multiplication factors of the reading. Besides the capabilities of reading resistance in the circuit, the volt-ohmmeter should also contain measurements for both AC and DC volts. Usually a range of zero to 250 volts is adequate.

Once a volt-ohmmeter has been acquired, tests can be made for various aspects of any appliance. To operate the volt-ohmmeter, attach probes according to the manufacturer's instructions. Select the proper scale as indicated in the troubleshooting sections of this book, and attach the volt-ohmmeter probes to the connections indicated in the testing section of the book.

For example, if the power cord is being tested, the volt-ohmmeter would be set to the RX 1 scale. Jumper wires would be connected to the appliance end of the power cord and the volt-ohmmeter probes would be attached to the power cord prongs. If the cord is in proper condition, the volt-ohmmeter needle should move to the right, indicating zero ohms. If not, the power cord should be replaced. There are several tests where the reading of the volt-ohmmeter is important, such as testing a heating coil. This is where the difference exists between the volt-ohmmeter and the continuity tester. The latter can only tell if the lines are open, not if the proper amount of resistance exists in the component.

The volt-ohmmeter can also indicate both AC and DC voltage. With the properly rated volt-ohmmeter in the position indicating 120 to 240 AC volts, volt-ohmmeter probes can be inserted into the wall outlet. If the outlet is carrying voltage, the meter will not only indicate the presence of voltage but also the amount of voltage. When testing the voltage drop in wall outlets, which is important to the proper function of many appliances, the volt-ohmmeter will be able to indicate any potential problems. With the indicator turned to DC voltage reading, the volt-ohmmeter can be used to trace voltage in circuits and operate as a battery tester.

Supplies Required

Repairing appliances calls for tools, know-how, *and* the proper supplies

The first thing a home repair person should have handy is contact cleaner. A few sprays of contact cleaner on switch contacts, according to manufacturer's instructions, will almost bring the switch back to new again. It is also wise to include contact cleaning as part of an annual maintenance program.

Also important are wire connections. When possible, professional appliance repair persons use crimp connectors. Instead of soldering wires to terminals, a crimp connector is attached to the exposed wire using the multipurpose tool. Once in place, the terminal can be screwed into position. If two wires are to be spliced together, electrical tape should be used to protect the connection.

A multipurpose grease and a light oil should also be on hand to lubricate moving appliance parts.

Appendix C

Tricks of the Trade

Where to Obtain Specs

A professional repair person can make a repair appear as if a child could perform the same task. However, as many do-it-yourselfers have found, watching someone who knows what he or she is doing fix an appliance and doing it yourself are two different things. The real difference is not so much who is making the repair as it is knowing the little tricks that make the job go so much easier. Tricks of the trade make the difference between a professional and a less informed do-it-yourselfer.

One of the initial steps in becoming aware of professional hints is to know the most probable malfunction an appliance may have. When the professional repair person begins a job, he or she seems to know exactly where

313

the problem lies, to the amazement of those looking on. The trick is to follow the troubleshooting flow charts provided in Sections I and II in this book. Although the professional repair person may not open a troubleshooting guide in front of the customer, the professional follows the same procedures from having used the troubleshooting chart early in his or her career. By using the charts frequently, most individuals can soon commit the steps to memory.

Troubleshooting charts will tell you where the problem is and then how to make the necessary repair. However, there are two situations that can spoil the do-it-yourselfer's repair job: not being able to identify and remove a malfunctioned part and not being able to find a replacement part.

In following the troubleshooting guide, the repair person is told when and how to check a component. Since each appliance is different in design, the repair person must locate the component in the appliance. For the professional who works on the same models time and time again, locating the component is probably not a problem. For the person who repairs appliances less frequently, frustration can set in.

Even the less-experienced appliance repair person need not become frustrated when searching for components in the appliance. The illustrations in Sections I and II of this book provide an exploded view of each appliance, giving an approximate location of the component. Before beginning a repair, contact the manufacturer's customer assistance department and obtain an exploded view of your appliance. Such an illustration will give you basically two types of information: you will have a complete map of the appliance, illustrating every component, and a picture of what the component looks like. Before sending for the view, check the material normally sent with delivery of a new appliance. Many times manufacturers will send the exploded view along with the appliance.

With the malfunctioned component identified and removed from the appliance, the next task is to find the replacement part. The professional repair person would have the part in the truck, while the do-it-yourselfer might not know where to obtain it. There really is no problem. Another trick professionals use is to obtain all the information about the malfunctioned component. Most manufacturers have a parts listing and have the part available to the general public, either directly or through local dealers. There are specialty shops that also stock parts for appliances. Check the classified listings in the telephone book for a shop in your area.

Be aware, however, that you will probably require information about the part before purchasing the replacement component. Most parts will have a part number attached to the body of the unit. To be sure, check the exploded view of the appliance as supplied by the manufacturer. This illustration is another place where part numbers are listed. Once the part number has been identified, the component can be retrieved through the system already set up by the manufacturer.

New parts are always safer to purchase than used components. The manufacturer will usually give a warranty with the new part. However, if the appliance is fairly old, parts can sometimes be obtained from junkyards. Many times when new machines are purchased, the old machine is discarded. Since the old appliance probably was repaired during use, there is an excellent chance that there are fairly new parts in the appliance which can easily be reused. Finding the used part can be a problem. The do-it-yourselfer will have to locate an appliance made by the same manufacturer around the same time as his or her appliance was made. In this case, the component part number must be identical. Unless the do-it-yourselfer finds a junked appliance right away, buying the new part might be the right move.

Tricks to Installing Parts

After the replacement part is in hand, the next task is to install it into the appliance, which is sometimes more difficult than it sounds. There are two basic methods of installing a component: by soldering the connections or by using solderless terminals and crimping the connections. Each method is used under certain circumstances, and each is not applicable to every connection.

The traditional method of making tight, proper connections is soldering. (See Illustration C-1.) Unfortunately, many people find soldering a little difficult. Soldering is the melting of a light metal called solder. As the solder melts, the liquid metal flows over the two wires to be connected. Within a few seconds, the metal solidifies, securing the connection. The trick to soldering is in the location of the heat. Beginners are frequently seen heating the solder, which leaves much of the solder on the soldering iron and little, if any, on the wires. After the wires have been twisted together, the soldering iron heats the wires, not the solder. With the wires heated, solder is then applied to the connection and the wires melt the solder.

Whenever a terminal connection of an appliance is not a screw-type contact, solder can, and should, be employed. Besides solder, a relatively new type of method to secure a connection has been developed using solderless terminals or crimp connections. As the name implies, there is no need to heat any wires or use solder. Each end of the wire is fitted with a crimp terminal. After the wire insulation is bared, the crimp terminal is slipped onto the exposed wire. (See Illustration C-2.) With the multipurpose tool, the sides of the crimp terminal are fixed to the wire. Crimp wires are perfect for appliance repairs. Once the crimp terminal has been installed, the wires are connected by a screw contact. Removing and installing the wire or component becomes a simple task. There are also crimp connections for in-line splicing.

The do-it-yourselfer will at some time be replacing appliance plugs. In many cases this is a relatively simple task. However, some plugs must be installed by using the Underwriter's knot. To ensure that wires are secured in the plug, the special knot should be tied before connecting the wires to the terminals. Round plugs usually provide room for the knot. (See Illustration C-3.)

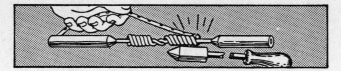

Applying solder. So solder will flow easier, first coat wires with electric soldering paste. With soldering iron, heat wires until solder melts and flows into every crevice.

Courtesy Sears, Roebuck and Co.

ILLUSTRATION C-1.

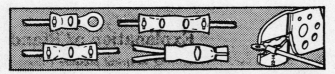

Solderless Terminals. Plastic insulation is permanently bonded to the terminal . . . cannot slip off or be removed. Install with one quick stroke of Sears Multi-Purpose Tool

Courtesy Sears, Roebuck and Co.

ILLUSTRATION C-2.

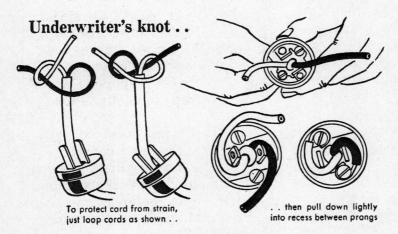

Underwriter's knot . .

To protect cord from strain, just loop cords as shown . .

. . then pull down lightly into recess between prongs

ILLUSTRATION C-3.

Tricks to Disassembling Appliances

Before opening any appliance, make sure the proper specifications are handy and be sure the power cord is unplugged. Manufacturers build appliances using the quickest and most economical connections available. However, when first looking at how to attack a disassembling job, these connections may leave the do-it-yourselfer puzzled.

Mainly in large appliances, smooth surfaces (tops, sides, backs) are held on by a spring clip. These clips usually cannot be seen. To remove the clips, insert a putty knife in the dividing groove or edge of the surface. Move the knife along the complete distance of the surface groove. The knife will be stopped by the spring clip. Once the clip has been found, center the knife on the clip, press in, and the clip should open. Continue the search for the clips since appliances usually have more than one spring clip.

Appliance handles are attached by a bolt groove arrangement. Bolts or screws are inserted into the handle. Once attached to the handle, bolts are inserted into keyhole-type holes on the appliance and pushed into the groove.

Another common method of attachment is the use of tabs, usually on the body of a plastic appliance. Use a screwdriver to separate body parts.

Frequently appliances will be manufactured using common fasteners. However, the heads of the fasteners are not easily seen. Many times screws are concealed under metal or cloth, or they are plugged or capped. To locate the fasteners, examine the appliance for a logical connection location or refer to the exploded view. Remove the cap, metal cover, or plug and disassemble according to common practice.

How to Talk Like A Professional

The difference between a professional repair person and an uninformed do-it-yourselfer is knowing the jargon of the trade. The following list gives the common terms used in the field and their meanings:

- *AC:* Alternating current, the type of power used in home wiring systems.
- *Ampere:* The unit of measuring electrical rate of flow.
- *Circuit:* Two or more wires through which electricity flows out from the source of supply to one or more outlets and then back.
- *Circuit breaker:* Performs the same function as a fuse in the service panel.
- *Color coding:* Identification of wires by color throughout the system to help ensure that hot wires will be connected only to hot wires and that neutral wires will run in a continuous, uninterrupted connection back to the ground terminal.
- *Conductors:* Common trade term for electric wires.
- *DC:* Direct current; used in some appliances.
- *Electric service panel:* The main panel through which electricity is brought into the house and then distributed to various branch circuits. Contains the main disconnect switch for the entire wiring system as well as fuses or circuit breakers.
- *Fuse:* A safety device that breaks the flow of electricity whenever a circuit becomes overloaded.
- *Grounding:* Connection of electrical system to the earth, a precaution necessary to prevent damage from lightning and to minimize danger from shocks.
- *Horsepower:* One horsepower = 746 watts.
- *Hot wires:* The power-carrying wires, usually black or red.
- *Insulation:* A protective sheathing used over wires to prevent escape of electricity.
- *Outlet:* A device that permits tapping of electricity at convenient locations for lights or appliances.
- *Receptacle:* A type of outlet to which electric cords can conveniently be plugged in.
- *Short circuit:* An improper connection between hot wires or between hot wires and a neutral wire.

Courtesy Sears, Roebuck and Co.

- *Switch:* A device for breaking or changing the flow of current.
- *Volt:* The unit of measuring electrical pressure.
- *Voltage drop:* A term used to indicate the voltage loss that occurs when wires are overloaded. Always make sure that any wires you install are of sufficiently heavy gauge to efficiently carry the electrical load for all appliances.
- *Watt:* The measurement showing current drain.

Amperes × Volts = Watts

Courtesy Sears, Roebuck and Co.

A

Appliance operation:
blender, 14
clothes dryer, 209
coffeemaker, 26
cooker, 34
dehumidifier, 221
dishwasher, 229
electric blanket, 40
electric broiler, 48
electric can opener, 56
electric clock, 67
electric curlers, 75
electric corn popper, 85
electric fan, 119
electric iron, 151
electric mixer, 165
electric knife, 93
electric shaver, 105
electric toothbrush, 113
handheld hair dryer, 129
heating pads, 137
hot plates, 143
humidifier, 247
refrigerator, 255
sewing machine, 265
space heater, 177
stove, 273
toaster, 185
washing machine, 281
waste disposer, 291
vacuum cleaner, 197

B

Blender, diagnosing, 17
Blender, operation, 14

C

Coffeemaker, diagnosing, 29
Coffeemaker, operation, 26
Cooker, diagnosing, 37
Cooker, operation, 34

D

Diagnosing:
blender, 17
coffeemaker, 29
cooker, 37
electric blanket, 43
electric broiler, 51
electric can opener, 59
electric clock, 69
electric curlers, 77
electric corn popper, 87
electric fan, 121
electric iron, 153
electric mixer, 167
electric knife, 95
electric shaver, 107
electric toothbrush, 113
handheld hair dryer, 131

heating pads, 139
hot plates, 145
humidifier, 249
refrigerator, 257
sewing machine, 267
space heater, 179
stove, 275
toaster, 187
washing machine, 283
waste disposer, 293
vacuum cleaner, 199

E

Electric blanket, diagnosing, 43
Electric blanket, operation, 40
Electric broiler, diagnosing, 51
Electric broiler, operation, 48
Electric can opener, diagnosing, 59
Electric can opener, operation, 56
Electric clock, diagnosing, 69
Electric clock, operation, 67
Electric curlers, diagnosing, 77
Electric curlers, operation, 75
Electric corn popper, diagnosing, 87
Electric corn popper, operation, 85
Electric fan, diagnosing, 121
Electric fan, operation, 119
Electric iron, diagnosing, 153
Electric iron, operation, 151
Electric mixer, diagnosing, 167
Electric mixer, operation, 165
Electric knife, diagnosing, 95
Electric knife, operation, 93
Electric shaver, diagnosing, 107
Electric shaver, operation, 105
Electric toothbrush, diagnosing, 115
Electric toothbrush, operation, 113
Electricity, tips, 296

H

Handheld hair dryer, diagnosing, 131
Handheld hair dryer, operation, 129
Heating pad, diagnosing, 139

Heating pad, operation, 137
Hot plate, diagnosing, 145
Hot plate, operation, 143
Humidifier, diagnosing, 249
Humidifier, operation, 247

1-Horse Power = 746 watts

L

Large appliance repair, 207

R

Refrigerator, diagnosing, 257
Refrigerator, operation, 255

S

Small appliance repair, 13
Sewing machine, diagnosing, 267
Sewing machine, operation, 265
Space heater, diagnosing, 179
Space heater, operation, 177
Stove, diagnosing, 275
Stove, operation, 273

T

Timesaving tips, 5
Toaster, diagnosing, 187
Toaster, operation, 185
Tools of trade, 308
Tricks of trade, 313

V

Vacuum cleaner, diagnosing, 199
Vacuum cleaner, operation, 197

W

Washing machine, diagnosing, 283
Washing machine, operation, 281
Waste disposer, diagnosing, 293
Waste disposer, operation, 291